PIE IN THE SKY

Other books by Irving Werstein

THIS WOUNDED LAND:
The Era of Reconstruction, 1865–1877

THE GREAT STRUGGLE:
Labor in America

LABOR'S DEFIANT LADY:
The Life of Mother Jones

PIE IN THE SKY
An American Struggle
THE WOBBLIES AND THEIR TIMES
by IRVING WERSTEIN
DELACORTE PRESS / NEW YORK

Published by
Dell Publishing Co., Inc.
750 Third Avenue
New York, New York 10017

Library of Congress Catalog Card Number: 69-18437
Manufactured in the United States of America

Design by BARBARA LIMAN

First printing

This book is for

BETTINA and GUY GRESFORD,

fair dinkum cobbers.

You will eat, bye and bye,
In that glorious land above the sky;
Work and pray, live on hay,
You'll get pie in the sky,
When you die!

CHORUS OF "The Preacher and the Slave,"
AN IWW SONG BY JOE HILL.

Preface

BACK IN THE 1920's when I was attending a public grammar school in Richmond Hill, Long Island, the custodian, a salty character, used to fascinate some of us with tales of his adventures as a Wobbly organizer. To me, Vincent St. John, Joe Hill, Big Bill Haywood, and Gurley Flynn were reincarnations of Robin Hood, his merry men, and the Maid Marian.

It was a time when stirring events such as the Paterson strike and the Lawrence and the Palmer raids were not yet obscured under the dust of history. Workingmen still sang Wobbly songs. Some wept when Big Bill died in Moscow. I knew people who had attended the Paterson Strike Pageant in Madison Square Garden. I even knew some who had been in free-speech fights out west.

The Wobblies always have had a place in my heart. Today, with college students and youth generally in a state of turmoil and dissent, I am reminded of the Wobblies—those gallant rebels who long ago shook the Establishment to its foundations. Earnest students demanding "academic freedom" are not on the same economic level as the "working stiffs" and "bindle stiffs" of yore, but, I believe, the campus rebels would have participated in the Wobbly-led free-speech fights.

Today's fractious young people also share youth with the Wobblies. Most of the men and women who once carried red cards were in their early twenties and thirties. Many still were teen-agers.

The past, the present, and the future are links in history's chain. After reading about young workingmen and women who clung to a "glorious dream," today's rebels might pause to ponder that the freedom's flame was lighted a long time ago; that dissension is an old American tradition; and that the so-called "Now" generation might well pay respect to the trailblazers of the past.

In this book, my purpose has not been to glorify the Wobblies but merely to tell their story "like it was." However, if a reader draws a present-day parallel, I will be well pleased.

I wish to thank those who helped me while I was working on *Pie in the Sky*. As always, the librarians at the New-York Historical Society were courteous and efficient. I must give my thanks to the late Captain John G. Sturges, a merchant mariner who recounted numerous stories of the Wobblies he had known, both the leaders and the rank and file. Henry Chafetz and Sidney B. Solomon, of the Pageant Book Co., provided me with much out-of-print material on the Wobblies and unionism in general.

I owe a debt of gratitude to my editor, Mr. George Nicholson, for his patience; to my agent, Miss Candida Donadio, for her guidance; to my wife for her uncomplaining cooperation; to my teen-age son for steering clear while my workroom door was closed.

I. W.

New York, October, 1968

Contents

A GLOWING DREAM

On tuesday morning, June 27, 1905, Chicago was host to a convention that had been called for an unusual reason. More than two hundred delegates and spectators crowded Brand's Hall, a shabby auditorium located on North Clark Street, for the opening session of the conclave.

Those at the meeting had traveled to Chicago from all corners of the country. Although many in that audience had deep political convictions, none were politicians. Even a casual onlooker could tell that this was not an assemblage of ward heelers, clubhouse hangers-on, party hacks, the typical crowds that gathered at conventions of big political parties.

The men and women in Brand's Hall that summery Tuesday in June were not there to pick a candidate for office. They had come together for something more idealistic than an election campaign. The delegates represented 60,000 workers organized in thirty-four national, state, or district trade unions. Miners, millworkers, bakers, brewers, lumberjacks, machinists—skilled and unskilled—had sent people to the meeting. Those present had little in common except their dedication to the labor movement and trade unionism. Their political backgrounds varied as widely as their occupations. Among them were socialists, anarchists, freethinkers, and assorted radicals and reformers. One newsman at the opening session noted: "Never before has such a collection been brought together under a single roof. . . ."

A "collection" it was.

On the speakers' dais sat a tall, black-bearded Roman Catholic priest named Thomas J. Hagerty, who edited a labor newspaper. Next to him was Eugene Victor Debs, union organizer and head of the American Socialist Party. Debs had been the Socialist nominee for President of the United States in 1900 and 1904. (In his time, he also would run for the presidency in 1908, 1912, and 1920.)

On Debs' left was one of the labor movement's most colorful figures, a spunky, seventy-five-year-old lady, Mary "Mother" Jones. Clad in quaint, old-fashioned clothes, she looked like a kindly grandmother, an illusion strengthened by her curly white hair and gentle gray eyes that peered softly through silver-rimmed spectacles. However, Mother Jones's appearance was deceptive.

She had a well-deserved reputation as a militant leader who had been in the van of the most fiercely contested strikes in American history. By 1905, she was a veteran unionist, with more than thirty-five years of experience in the labor movement. The grandmotherly woman had been jailed, shot at, and beaten in the course of nearly four decades on the labor front.

After the death of her husband and four small children during the 1867 yellow-fever epidemic in Memphis, Tennessee, Mary Jones devoted her life to the union cause. So dedicated to it was she that the workers nicknamed her "Mother" at a time when that word was revered. This was the workers' way of expressing the love and respect they felt for her.

(Mother Jones lived until 1930; she was one hundred years and six months old at the time of her death. Her funeral was attended by more than 20,000 union workers. The cortege stretched for two miles behind the hearse that bore her to Mt. Olive Cemetery, in Illinois, where she was buried alongside union miners she had led in many strikes.)

Another female labor celebrity on the platform was Mrs. Lucy Parsons, the widow of Albert R. Parsons, who had died on the gallows after an 1886 Chicago labor riot.

Known to history as the Haymarket Affair, that violent incident was touched off when a bomb exploded in the ranks of policemen guarding an anarchist street meeting. The blast killed one officer, wounded many others, and sparked a shooting affray between the police and the crowd. Scores were injured and a number killed on both sides. Blame for the bombing was pinned on the anarchists and eight of their leaders were arrested. In a singularly prejudiced trial, five defendants received death sentences, while three got life imprisonment. Four of the condemned men died on the gallows; the fifth committed suicide in his cell.

(In 1893, the Haymarket survivors were granted full pardon by John Peter Altgeld, the liberal governor of Illinois, who believed the anarchists had not received a fair trial. Altgeld's political career was damaged by this decision, but he insisted that freeing the anarchists was the only decent course open to him. "I refuse to stand silent in the face of injustice," he declared.)

After her husband's execution, Lucy Parsons, like Mother Jones, gave herself to the labor movement. She was indefatigable, writing articles, addressing meetings, serving on committees, fighting against child labor and other abuses, selflessly expending time and energy in the struggle to win a better life for the American workers.

Also on the platform was the country's best-known left-wing orator, Curaçao-born Daniel De Leon. A self-styled genius, De Leon was admired as a speaker and detested as a man by his fellow radicals. Although acknowledged by experts to be the foremost interpreter of socialist theory in the United States, De Leon, a cantankerous, argumentative and willful individual, had more foes than friends within the labor movement.

Fired for radicalism in 1889 from a teaching post at Columbia University, the embittered De Leon fully turned his substantial talents and intellect to the study and practice of socialism. Soon, his difficult personality caused deep problems for him within the Socialist Party (SP), and when that body rejected certain of his views, De Leon walked out to join a dissident, splinter group, the Socialist Labor Party (SLP). Very quickly he rose to the leadership of that small organization whose members slavishly followed and accepted everything he set forth. This reverence puffed De Leon's already swollen ego. "I have disciples, not comrades," he boasted.

At the time of the Chicago convention, De Leon was espousing the opinion that American trade unionists should be involved in politics as well as economics. "We must attack the capitalists on every front," he preached. "The workers must enter the political lists and put forth candidates for every office both locally and nationally. Only in this way can we break the capitalist grip on society; by winning at the polls as well as by gaining control of the industries."

To some extent, this was a new concept for the American working class, although in Europe labor parties had existed for decades. In 1905, except for those who voted for Socialist or Socialist Labor Party candidates, American radicals had spurned what they called "bourgeois" politics. From time to time working-class parties such as the Workingman's Association, the Populists, and the Greenback Party appeared on the ballot only to disappear after a brief existence. The great mass of American workers supported either the Republicans or the Democrats. Then, as now, the United States was essentially a two-party country.

The influential and powerful American Federation of Labor (AFL) shunned political ties. Occasionally, AFL leaders urged their followers to back "friends of labor," but the AFL would go no further, limiting its role to fight for more pay and better working conditions for the skilled workers who made up its membership.

(While De Leon completely dominated the SLP, he carried little weight with workers outside the party. When the SLP nominated him for the governorship of New York in 1904, he polled only a disappointing 14,651 votes. That same year, Eugene Debs, running for president on the Socialist Party ticket, garnered some 400,000 votes. The SLP had no mass support despite De Leon's brilliance; however, under the common-sense leadership of Eugene Debs, the Socialist Party was gaining ground. With a total of 13,000,000 voters in 1904, 400,000 votes were significant in a tight election. Republican and Democratic Party chieftains were growing concerned over the "increasing radicalism infecting the country" and began to take seriously, as a third-party threat, Debs and the Socialists.)

Besides Debs, Lucy Parsons, Father Hagerty, Mother Jones, and De Leon, many other well-known labor personages appeared at Brand's Hall. There were union heads, rank and filers, labor newspaper editors, scores of men and women tested under fire on innumerable picket lines, when violence marred the industrial landscape, during the 1890's and early 1900's.

If the delegates differed widely on means of solving the difficulties and problems of the American working class, they were in solid agreement that the AFL was a dismal failure. The AFL was concerned only with the well-being of skilled workers organized in separate craft unions. The federation had no regard for the many thousands of unskilled workers, Negro workers, and women workers.

Samuel Gompers, the president of the AFL, once said, "The unskilled are impossible to organize. . . . We can't be bothered with them, nor must we become involved in such side issues as the problems of the Negroes and the inequities facing female labor. . . . Our first and only duty is to those who belong to our unions, the skilled craftsmen of America. . . . The unskilled are as albatrosses dangling from the neck of the labor movement. . . ."

The delegates in Brand's Hall saw matters differently. They believed that every worker—skilled or unskilled; black or white; male or female—should be enrolled in a union. They also had different ideas about how unions should function. Instead of three, four, or even more unions in a single industry, the delegates felt that all workers in the same industry should belong to the same "industrial" union, no matter how high or how humble his job.

In the AFL, where "craft" unions prevailed, workers doing different jobs within the same industry belonged to separate unions. For instance, in the building trades, there were unions for plumbers, plasterers, carpenters, stonemasons, lathers, electricians, and painters, all working on the same job. If one union went on strike, the others were not bound to support the walkout. The same situation prevailed in factories that employed several categories of workers. AFL unions lacked solidarity and unity; each was in business for itself and the workers under its jurisdiction.

Industrial unions, as opposed to craft unions, assured working-class unity. Workers organized along industrial lines could stand together in a labor dispute. If a strike was called, every man, woman, and child (children of fourteen and even younger worked in factories during the early 1900's) in the shop, or even the whole industry, would walk off the job.

Despite the apparent advantages of industrial unions over craft unions, the AFL leadership refused to permit organizational changes. As a result, backers of industrial unions long had fought the oligarchy of the AFL. In some cases, these "militants" had been expelled from the federation—not only individuals, but also entire local and national unions.

The attitude of the AFL created at least one rival labor federation. Known at first as the Western Labor Union (WLU), it later was renamed the American Labor Union (ALU). Although small, the ALU, by its very existence, irked Gompers and his conservative cohorts.

The backbone of the ALU was the 27,000-man Western Federation of Miners. The ALU's newspaper was edited by the priest, Father Hagerty, an unbridled maverick who was completely fearless.

Once he was warned that if he addressed a certain strike meeting, hired company thugs would "beat his brains out." Undeterred, Father Hagerty went to the rally, mounted the podium, reached under his coat, and pulled out a pair of Colt six-shooters. Scowling out at the crowd, the black-bearded priest set the revolvers on the lectern and announced, "If there's any man here who has in mind to do me bodily harm, I'm warning him that I can hit a dime at twenty paces, shooting with either hand. Believe me, putting a bullet between a man's eyes is a lot easier. If you doubt me, you'd better make peace with God right now." He paused and eyed the silent throng. "Now, if you don't mind, I'll get on with my speech." Father Hagerty spoke without interruption. The company's hoodlums made neither a sound nor a hostile move.

After the meeting a striker asked Father Hagerty whether he actually would have shot at an assailant.

"No, my son," the priest said. "I'd not have shot *at* him! I'd have blown off the top of his head!"

Father Hagerty was unique, but only because he was a priest. Other unionists were just as militant and just as strongly opposed to the AFL as he.

In November, 1904, six anti-AFL union men met in Chicago to discuss what might be done to correct the flaws in the labor movement. These half-dozen concerned men included Clarence Smith, secretary of the ALU; Father Hagerty; George Estes and W. L. Hall, of the United Brotherhood of Railway Employees; Isaac Cowan, Amalgamated Society of Engineers, which just had been thrown out of the AFL; and William Trautmann, who edited the German-language weekly of the brewery workers. Collaborating closely with Eugene Debs and other militants, the six rebels put out a call to a larger conference in January, 1905, which was attended by more anti-AFL unionists.

The January meeting decided upon a full-scale convention to be held during June, 1905, with delegates from all unions and labor groups adhering to the belief that "the working class, if correctly organized on both political and industrial lines" had the ability "to take possession of and operate successfully . . . the industries of the country. . . ."

The summons to the June conference also called upon the working class to "overthrow capitalism" and replace it with a vaguely defined, utopian "Co-operative Commonwealth" in which the wage system would be abolished, bosses eliminated, and workers enabled "to enjoy the fruits of their toil."

Rarely had any gathering in the United States ever before been attended by so many idealists, dreamers, and visionaries as was the one that met on June 27, 1905, in Brand's Hall, Chicago. Out of this meeting came a new labor federation, the most dynamic, democratic, and idealistic in American history. It was called the Industrial Workers of the World (IWW), more commonly known as the "Wobblies."

(The origin of the name "Wobbly" in reference to the IWW never has been definitely traced, although several versions crop up from time to time. The most unlikely one concerns a waiter in a Chinese restaurant who asked, "All loo eye wobble wobble?" meaning "Are you IWW?" when serving a group of IWW members.

The Wobblies flourished for a time, not only in the United States, but also in Australia, Great Britain, and Canada, where the IWW took hold among the workers.

If the new organization had good friends, it also had bitter enemies who saw the Wobblies as dangerous radicals, a revolutionary vanguard that had to be destroyed. The IWW's foes existed both inside and outside the labor movement. Industrialists and employers met the Wobblies with violence. IWW organizers were beaten, framed, jailed, and in one case, at least, executed by the state of Utah on a trumped-up murder charge. At various times, Wobblies met cruel deaths at the hands of lynch mobs and assassins.

The AFL fought the IWW by breaking Wobbly-led strikes, by smear campaigns, and by terror. AFL "goons" smashed IWW headquarters and manhandled individual Wobblies. The press waged an intensive and unrelenting propaganda war on the IWW. Newspapers took every opportunity to denounce the Wobblies in print. According to the dailies, the initials IWW stood for "I Won't Work" or "I Want Whiskey." They labeled Wobblies as "bums," "hoboes," "drifters," "anarchists," "reds," "traitors," and "riffraff."

Despite all the forces arrayed against it, the Industrial Workers of the World captured the imagination of the American working class to such an extent that, during the years the IWW was at its peak, nearly one million laboring men and women carried a so-called "red card," the color of the IWW membership card. However, the turnover in the IWW was high and there probably were never more than 150,000 to 200,000 members at one time.

Although they failed in their ultimate aim as revolutionaries and their Co-operative Commonwealth remained a visionary's dream, the Wobblies left an indelible impact on the American social order. A whole generation sang the songs composed by Wobbly bards such as Joe Hill, Ralph Chaplin, and a colorful character known only as T-Bone Slim. The Wobblies added to American slang; their expressions are still in use. They created and popularized terms such as "flunkey," "hep cat," "haywire," and "fink."

American folk music owes much to Wobbly composers. Joe Hill's "The Preacher and the Slave" is in every folksinger's repertoire. The unknown Wobbly who composed "Hallelujah I'm a Bum" would be pleased to know that his rollicking song is still heard. Even today, every union man knows Ralph Chaplin's stirring picket-line marching song, "Solidarity Forever."

A historian said of the Wobblies: "If nothing more, these fervent people believed deeply in the future of the working class . . . and the hope of a better world. . . ."

Their faith was summed up in a verse by the Wobbly poet, Ralph Chaplin:

For we have a glowing dream
Of how fair the world will seem
When each man can live life
Secure and free . . .

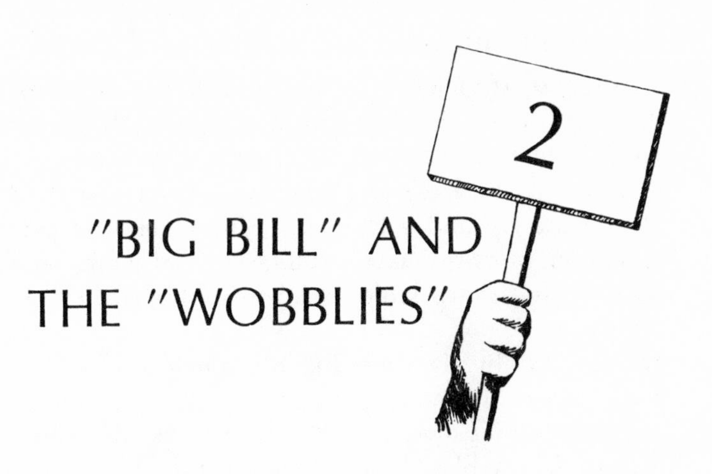

2

"BIG BILL" AND THE "WOBBLIES"

THE FIRST ATTEMPT to achieve Chaplin's "glowing dream" started in Brand's Hall at 10:00 A.M., June 27, 1905, when a powerfully built giant of a man shambled to the rostrum. Lacking a gavel, he thumped the lectern with a piece of board and boomed, "Fellow workers, I now call this meeting to order!"

It was fitting and proper that William Dudley Haywood should be the convention keynoter. At thirty-six, Big Bill, as he was known, had long been a rebel on the side of society's underdogs. In 1905, Haywood, whose rugged face reminded one reporter of a "scarred battlefield," was the secretary of the Western Federation of Miners (WFM). The men of the WFM regarded him as a hero. Almost singlehandedly, Big Bill had organized and led them to victory in a series of strikes that won higher pay and improved working conditions for the miners.

Born February 4, 1869, at Salt Lake City, Utah, then part of the crude, primitive frontier, Bill Haywood grew up in an atmosphere of violence. When Big Bill was three, his father died, and he was reared by his mother, who had come to the United States as a young girl from South Africa.

At seven, the lad had already witnessed a fatal shooting, bloody brawls, and a lynching. Misfortune overtook young Haywood; he was making a slingshot and while carving the wood with a sharp knife, accidently blinded himself in the right eye.

This disability brought Big Bill much trouble. "Hardly a week passed," he later wrote, "without a fight with some boy or other who called me 'Deadeye Dick' or 'Squint Eye' because of my blind eye." However, this did not impose as much of a hardship on him as it might seem. "I liked to fight," Haywood added significantly.

At the age of nine, his schooling terminated. In order to help support his widowed mother, Big Bill went to work as a bellhop in a Salt Lake City hotel. A succession of jobs followed: theater usher, store clerk, messenger, and farm-hand. It was while working for a farmer that Haywood pulled his first strike. The farmer, an ill-tempered man, struck the boy with a whip. Bill promptly gathered his belongings and went home. "No man can treat a worker that way and expect him to continue working," the boy said.

At fifteen, Haywood took a job as a copper miner in Nevada. But within a few years, he switched from mining and started afresh on a homestead to try his hand at farming and ranching.

(Under the Homestead Act of 1862, the U.S. government offered a man forty acres in a specified territory. If the recipient built a house and cultivated the land for five years, the homestead became his property. The government encouraged this sort of settlement to attract people into the open spaces of the West and Southwest.)

Big Bill's homestead stake was in Nevada; he enjoyed the

life, liked the work, and got along well with farmers, cowboys, and ranchers. Married to pretty teen-aged Jane Minor, Haywood believed he was building a fine, secure future for his bride and himself.

But all was not smooth in the Haywood home. After bearing two daughters, Jane Haywood fell ill and became a semi-invalid. Big Bill lost his homestead before the five-year period was up, when the government decided to use his land as part of an Indian reservation. This embittered Big Bill. He resented going back to the mines for a living. After he had tasted independence, the shackles of what he termed "wage slavery" irked him. This was a feeling common among many of his fellow miners. Men raised in the West had a burning spirit of independence. The region had been opened by trappers, traders, homesteaders, ranchers, and prospectors accustomed to working for themselves, not for others.

That tradition still prevailed in the region, but the day of such individual endeavor was drawing to an end. Great and powerful corporations—mining companies, lumber trusts, and ranch syndicates—were driving out the small operators. The erstwhile independents seethed at losing their freedom. Small wonder that, with such militant workers, a fighting union like the Western Federation of Miners was formed. The conservative AFL, with its mild tactics, could not satisfy the spirited Westerners.

Big Bill Haywood rose rapidly in the WFM by showing his leadership talents during the hard-fought, bloody strikes the union launched in Colorado against copper, lead, zinc, and tin-mine operators. Haywood's quick mind, oratorical skill, and raw courage made him a legend among the metal miners.

Now, Big Bill, standing before the delegates in Brand's Hall, cried, "This meeting is the Continental Congress of the

Working Class!" The one-eyed labor veteran was exaggerating. He gave the convention more importance than it merited, but nobody in his audience cared. They wildly cheered his words.

Haywood more accurately described the purpose of the gathering when he stated "We are here today . . . to confederate the workers . . . into a working class movement that shall have for its goal the emancipation of the working class from the slave bondage of capitalism. . . ."

Again cheers rocked the hall. The delegates were with Big Bill all the way, but differed on the means of achieving his revolutionary aim.

However, there was complete unanimity that the AFL never could emancipate the working class or that it indeed intended to do so. The AFL had not even succeeded in enlisting a majority of American workers into unions. Only five percent of the working people in the United States belonged to any union. The rest, unorganized, were incapable of protecting their own interests.

Among these were black workers who faced the cruel discrimination that always had been their lot in America. The AFL also scorned the later immigrants from southern and eastern Europe—skilled, unskilled, and semiskilled workers. These recent arrivals, most of them unable to speak English or even to cope with problems arising from the complex American industrial society, were especially vulnerable on the labor market.

Highly skilled blacks and foreigners also were victimized. Not only did AFL craft unions deny them membership, but native-born Americans regarded them with suspicion and hatred. The employers shrewdly exploited the animosities among native, foreign-born, and black workers. If AFL craftsmen went on strike, the bosses hired blacks or foreigners as strikebreakers—at lower wages. Union demands for higher pay were throttled by the threat of employing blacks and "greenhorns," as immigrants were called. The refusal of AFL unions to open membership rolls to blacks and foreigners seriously impaired the progress of the American working class.

Big Bill made this one of the main points in his keynote address. Foreigners and blacks must be included in the new labor federation the delegates would create.

"I don't care a snap of my fingers whether or not the skilled workers join the industrial movement at this time," he said. "We're going down into the gutter to get at the mass of workers and bring them up to a decent plane of living."

One speaker after another repeated this pledge. They stressed the urgent need for industrial unionism. Work formerly done by craftsmen and artisans was being turned out by machinery. Industry was replacing skilled workers with semiskilled and unskilled labor trained only enough to run the machines.

"By the middle of the twentieth century, craft unions will be as extinct as the dodo bird. . . . The era of industrial unionism is at hand," one speaker predicted.

The delegates argued for ten days over the adoption of a constitution for which Father Hagerty wrote the preamble. This unusual priest, who hailed from New Mexico, had been converted to socialist philosophies even before his ordination in 1892. By 1903, Hagerty's activities among copper miners in Colorado brought him suspension from priestly duties. Although his association with the Church had been terminated, Hagerty insisted he still was a priest and continued to function as one.

Father Hagerty's opening sentence in the preamble to the IWW constitution came bluntly to the point: "The working class and the employing class have nothing in common."

The preamble, which trumpeted on in similar style, set off

a furious debate over a single word contained in its second paragraph, which read:

> Between these two classes a struggle must go on until all the toilers come together on the political as well as industrial field, and take and hold that which they produce by their labor through an economic organization of the working class.

The controversial word was "political."

Most of the Western delegates opposed taking "political action at the capitalist ballot box." They believed only in *direct* action—strikes, sabotage, work stoppages. Many of them were "vagabond" or "itinerant" workers who moved from job to job as whim or season dictated. These men, known as "bindle stiffs"—a "bindle" was a blanket roll containing personal belongings—seldom remained in one place long enough to meet residential requirements for voting. As a result, few of them ever had cast a ballot in a public election and probably would not have done so under any circumstances. To that breed, all politicians were "corrupt grafters."

Bindle stiffs were lumberjacks, railroad construction workers, farmhands, logging-camp cooks, or miners. Although unschooled, many bindle stiffs were articulate and well read. Opposed to all forms of government, they were fanatically committed to the creed of industrial unionism and direct action to further the ends of the working class. In Europe the proponents of this creed were called Anarcho-syndicalists, a designation rarely used here.

The bindle stiffs opposed not only Republican and Democratic politicians, but Socialists and Social Laborites as well. They sought to prevent the new organization—The Industrial Workers of the World, it had been grandiosely named—from being dominated either by the Socialist Party or the Social Labor Party.

Daniel De Leon, leader of the SLP, urged the delegates, in a long, impassioned speech, to approve the preamble's political clause. "Political action is a civilized means of seeking progress," he said, reminding the antipolitical faction that "Every class struggle is a political struggle."

Although the controversy swung pro and con, when a vote came, the political clause won by a large majority mainly because De Leon had packed the house with SLP delegates. However, the question of direct action versus political action nearly wrecked the IWW at its inception and caused rifts that never healed.

But for this difference of opinion, the delegates had few areas of disagreement. Almost unanimously they approved a constitution that provided for an organization based on democratic principles and geared to lead the working class into a more equitable social order.

Any wage earner could join the IWW, regardless of race, creed, sex, or occupation. It made no difference to the Wobblies whether a person was black or white, native-born or foreign. If an immigrant carried a paid-up union card from his native land, he was eligible for immediate membership in the IWW. Unlike AFL unions, initiation fees and dues were low.

Among the important clauses in the constitution was one that recommended the general strike as labor's most effective means of overthrowing the capitalist system. The IWW constitution also condemned militarism and provided for the exclusion of any applicant who belonged to the police or the militia.

To prepare for a social order run by the working class, the IWW set up thirteen departments corresponding to the major industries in the United States at that time. All unions connected with a particular industry came under the same department. This was known as the One Big Union principle. Theoretically, every industry in the country could be simultaneously paralyzed by a concerted strike of the thirteen

IWW departments. When the proper moment came, the One Big Union would lead the One Big Strike raising the slogan, "A hurt to one is a hurt to all!"

On paper, at least, the possibility of a national—even international—general strike existed. It could become a reality if the IWW recruited enough workers both in the United States and abroad. More visionary Wobblies saw the movement spreading around the world, so that the One Big Strike could cripple capitalism in every country.

As if to point up the internationalism of the IWW, the delegates rose at the end of the proceedings and closed the convention by singing the stirring anthem of left-wingers the world over—"The Internationale." The voices of the delegates especially emphasized the final words of the spirited song, prophetic words, they chose to believe:

> The earth shall rise on new foundations,
> We have been naught, we shall be all!

The notion of One Big Union leading the One Big Strike for the revolutionary purpose of overthrowing the capitalist system did not originate with the founders of the IWW. The Syndicalist Movement in Europe preached the gospel of General Strike and that the ultimate weapon was to paralyze industry and government.

This concept of working-class solidarity was first mentioned back in the early 1840's by Pierre Joseph Proudhon, a French scholar known as the "Father of Anarchism." Proudhon believed that the working class could take over in every country if the principles of One Big Union and One Big Strike were applied.

Naïvely enough, perhaps innocently, he also propounded the theory that when the workers did assume power there would be no one left to exploit and oppress. Therefore, the need for a government was eliminated and the state would "wither away." According to Proudhon, "Government of man by man in every form is oppression. The highest perfection of society is formed in the union of order and anarchy. . . ."

To a large extent the Wobblies subscribed to that sentiment.

THE STEUNENBERG MURDER AND AFTER

DESPITE RADICAL ORATORY and revolutionary songs, the founders of the IWW inexplicably elected the most conservative men in their midst to run the first General Executive Board (GEB). A right-wing Socialist, Charles Sherman, of the United Mine Workers, was made president. Bumbling William Trautmann, of the Brewers Union, was the most radical of the officers. Observers considered him to be as "tame as a kitten."

It was surprising that such men should have gained leadership in the IWW, since radicals apparently had dominated the convention. However, all was not as it seemed. The radicals made the most noise at Brand's Hall, but after ten days of long-winded debate, most delegates had grown restive. When it came to electing officers, the men best qualified for the posts were found to be unavailable. Debs was too closely connected with the Socialists as De Leon was with the SLP. Haywood's duties in the WFM kept him from holding office in the IWW. The bindle stiffs, led by Vincent St. John, a brilliant and militant radical, boycotted the elections because the convention had approved the political clause in the constitution.

Impatient to conclude the meeting, the delegates unanimously nominated and elected a slate of second-raters as officers and GEB members. The slapdash fashion in which the IWW chose its leadership soon caused serious difficulties.

The IWW ran into a storm of crises from its beginning. About six months after the first convention, Frank Steunenberg, formerly governor of Idaho, was murdered. A Democrat, Steunenberg had held office from 1897 to 1901 at a time when the Western Federation of Miners was conducting savagely contested strikes in Idaho. Steunenberg's anti-WFM actions earned him many enemies among the miners. Siding with the mine owners, the governor did everything possible to break the strikes. WFM officials and rank-and-file members openly expressed their hatred of him.

On December 30, 1905, the ex-governor, by then a prosperous sheepman, plodded through the snow to the mailbox outside his home. Opening the mailbox door, he was mortally wounded by a booby-trap bomb that had been concealed in the box.

The slaying aroused public wrath. The press baldly accused the WFM of instigating the murder to take revenge on Steunenberg. The wave of anger over the killing rose to such a pitch in Idaho that when a citizen's committee offered a $25,000 reward for the arrest and conviction of the culprits, Governor Frank R. Gooding added another $5,000 to the sum.

Soon after the murder, a man called Harry Orchard, whose real name was Albert E. Horsley, was arrested by James McParlan, chief of the Pinkerton Detective Agency's Denver office. (McParlan, a crack operative, was an "expert" in labor cases. Some twenty-five years earlier, he had penetrated a secret organization of coal miners in Pennsylvania. This group, known as the "Molly Maguires," was suspected of murdering several mine foremen during a strike. On the basis of McParlan's testimony, a number of Mollies were hanged. Some modern historians believe that the Mollies were executed on false evidence concocted by McParlan on behalf of the mine operators.)

Orchard, a small, rather affable man, once had belonged to the WFM and, at the time of his arrest, in January, 1906, claimed to be a sheep dealer. For reasons still unexplained, Orchard confessed to Steunenberg's murder.

The ex-governor's death, he alleged, had been plotted by an "inner circle" of WFM "radicals." Heading this elite group were Big Bill Haywood, the union's secretary; Charles Moyer, president of the WFM; and George Pettibone, a former WFM official. The trio, according to Orchard, "masterminded" the slaying of Steunenberg to "get even" with the ex-governor.

McParlan's agents in Denver kidnapped Moyer, Pettibone, and Haywood and rushed them to Boise, Idaho, in the dead of night, aboard a special train. Charged with "conspiracy to commit murder," the three union men were held in the death house of the Idaho State Penitentiary.

The high-handed seizure of Moyer, Pettibone, and Haywood outraged organized labor and a large segment of the American public. Not only the IWW and the WFM contributed to the prisoners' defense, but conservative AFL unions also chipped in to hire a lawyer and pay court expenses.

The Moyer-Pettibone-Haywood Defense Committee swiftly raised $10,000, a large sum in 1906, and used the money to engage Clarence Darrow, the country's most distinguished trial lawyer. Although he was ill, Darrow took on the case, which did not come to court until May, 1907.

Raising funds and rallying the labor movement to the support of the defendants was accomplished at a time when the

IWW was almost torn apart by internal problems and dissensions.

Between the initial June, 1905, convention and the second IWW convention, which originally had been scheduled for May, 1906, and then postponed until late September, the responsibility for conducting all organizational affairs lay with the elected officers and the GEB.

During the seventeen-month-long interval that separated the conventions, Charles Sherman's administration aroused much animosity in the ranks of the IWW. Although the Wobbly treasury was small, Sherman spent money with a free hand, including good-sized sums for "personal expenses" allegedly incurred "in the line of duty."

A fellow GEB member, William Trautmann, who supervised the IWW newspaper, *Industrial Worker*, proved incompetent for the job. "The thing Trautmann did best was to guzzle beer," a Wobbly recalled years later.

Under Sherman, the GEB exercised dictatorial powers, imposing its wishes on the membership in a manner that mocked the democratic principles upon which the IWW had been founded.

"Sherman was Czar and Trautmann his Crown Prince," a rank and filer noted. "The average Wobbly couldn't wait for the convention to give the GEB the heave-ho!"

The Second National Convention of the IWW convened September 17, 1906, at a hall on Halsted and Adams streets in Chicago. It was hectic and stormy from the outset. Rancor, acrimony, and hard feelings erupted on all sides when the delegates assembled.

Anti-Sherman sentiment was rampant and the embattled IWW president, backed by most of the GEB, resisted furiously. Daniel De Leon, of the SLP, headed the opposition. He had assumed that role only because more popular leaders such as Father Hagerty, Eugene Debs, and Big Bill Haywood were not at the convention. (Debs and Hagerty were ill; Haywood was in prison awaiting trial for the Steunenberg murder.)

De Leon's faction was bolstered by a defector from the ruling clique—beer-swilling William Trautmann, who had fallen out with Sherman. Between them, Trautmann and De Leon controlled a strong minority among the delegates. Sherman countered by having his handpicked credentials committee refuse to seat delegates known to be backers of De Leon.

Strong-arm men loyal to Sherman assisted the credentials committee and the convention's preliminaries were enlivened by arguments, hot words, and a few brawls. So many more delegates than had been expected sought entry into the meeting hall that larger quarters were needed. Brand's Hall, the birthplace of the IWW, was hired once again and the noisy conclave moved to the North Clark Street address.

If Sherman and his cohorts believed that their attempt to unseat De Leon's people would discourage the opposition, they were sorely disappointed. Instead of collapsing, the dissidents persisted and kept the convention in a turmoil for a week, until Sherman finally gave in and agreed to admit the De Leon group.

But even in his moment of victory, the SLP leader still had a hatful of troubles. The seven-day-long dispute had drained De Leon's followers of funds. Hungry, without shelter, they began to talk about going home. Actually, this had been part of Sherman's strategy. His supporters were receiving expense money of $1.50 per day (in 1906, this would buy three meals and a bed in a cheap boardinghouse). Sherman was aware that De Leon's supporters had little money. "We thought we could starve them out," he later admitted.

De Leon overcame his difficulties by calling on the convention to pay all certified delegates a $1.50 *per diem* allowance. The resolution passed despite violent objections from Sherman. The remainder of the convention was marked by successive defeats and rebuffs for Sherman, and he grew desperate as the clamor to remove him from office became more intense.

The De Leon-Trautmann faction gained an important recruit, Vincent St. John, a WFM organizer and a founder of the IWW. Thirty-three years old in 1906, St. John had come west from his native Kentucky. He was so dedicated to the WFM that the members dubbed him "The Saint."

If union men admired St. John, he reciprocated their feelings. His oft-repeated remark, "I'd give my life for the miners," almost came to pass in the late '90's, when The Saint ruined his lungs while leading to safety miners trapped in the smoke-filled passageways of a Telluride, Colorado, mine after an explosion.

St. John died at the age of fifty-six in 1929 and Joe Ettor, a fellow Wobbly, eulogized him in these words: "The Saint was at the heart of the labor movement. . . . The true story of labor's struggles over the past thirty years is the story of Vincent St. John. . . ."

When The Saint joined the forces against him, Sherman, on the verge of defeat, took the sort of direct action espoused by the Wobblies. With several faithful members of the GEB, he took over the IWW headquarters at 146 West Madison Street, Chicago. Incredibly, he hired guards from a notorious "Industrial Protective" agency that specialized in supplying strikebreakers, to keep members of the De Leon group out of the offices.

Sherman's action shocked most Wobblies. His use of professional scabs was inexplicable. As one observer wryly remarked, "I guess Charlie's like everyone else. There are times when a man must rise above his own principles!"

What followed next was of almost comic proportions.

When St. John learned what Sherman had done, he rushed to West Madison Street, accompanied by another dissident,

Frank Heslewood. The two men climbed up five flights of stairs to the IWW office only to be accosted at the top by a pair of burly guards.

"Don't come any farther," one of them shouted. "I know you, Saint, and you ain't welcome here!"

"You've no right to bar me," St. John argued. "I'm a member and an officer of this organization. These are our offices. I'm going in there."

"Like hell, you are!" the guard said, drawing a blackjack and slamming The Saint over the head with it.

Stunned, his head bleeding, St. John, aided by Heslewood, stumbled down the steps. "It was a case where discretion was the better part of valor," The Saint ruefully recalled.

His hasty departure saved him and Heslewood from arrest. Chicago police, responding to a call from Sherman's office, arrived just too late to nab the fleeing Wobblies.

After this episode, The Saint behaved in a manner totally alien to his past actions. He went to see a lawyer. This was especially ironical. Wobblies called lawyers "the judicial lackeys of the bosses." The man St. John consulted was Clarence Darrow, a known friend of labor, and the attorney for Moyer, Pettibone, and Haywood. According to The Saint, Sherman was "usurping" the IWW offices and "manipulating" the organization's funds.

Although Darrow was amused by the situation, he gave it his full attention and started court proceedings against Sherman. But before a judge could hand down a ruling, a union-wide referendum ousted Sherman. The deposed president refused to accept the verdict of the membership and, for some months, kept open the West Madison Street offices, although he had no business to conduct. After a time, Sherman surrendered the IWW files and correspondence and retired from the labor movement with ill grace.

Daniel De Leon presided over the IWW from an office at 212 Bush Terminal. The new GEB was made up mainly of direct actionists such as The Saint and Frank Heslewood. The radicals, who had failed to take over at the founding convention, gained complete control of the IWW a year later.

Had De Leon's rise and Sherman's downfall forged solidarity within the IWW, it would have been a worthy change. Instead, the power shift brought on even more serious dissension. Before long, it caused the withdrawal of the strongest union, the Western Federation of Miners, from the IWW.

For almost a decade, the WFM had been leading strike after strike in the mines and smelters of Colorado, Idaho, Nevada, Utah, and New Mexico. The union waged rough-and-tumble struggles. WFM strikes usually were marked by bloodshed on both sides. The leaders made little effort to negotiate with employers. A dispute invariably led to a walk-out. But after ten years, WFM members were beginning to wonder whether it was possible to strike less and bargain more. They were weary of picket lines and broken heads.

When De Leon and his radical followers took over the IWW, many WFM men were displeased. As one put it, "We weren't convinced that direct action was the best tactic to pursue. We also had our doubts about De Leon; to put it bluntly, we simply didn't trust him. We felt he was going to sell us out to the Socialist Labor Party."

There also was criticism of the way the De Leon-Trautmann-St. John group had jettisoned Sherman. John M. O'Neill, editor of the WFM official publication, the *Miners' Magazine,* editorially blasted De Leon, Trautmann, and The Saint.

"The IWW convention," O'Neill wrote, "degenerated into a mob. . . . I believe that the second convention was a conspiracy to resurrect the corpse of the Socialist Labor Party . . . and I strongly protest this misusage of the IWW. . . ."

O'Neill's piece triggered a split in the WFM. One faction favored St. John and the Wobblies; the other stood with

O'Neill and demanded that the miners quit the IWW. This argument caused a rift between Charles Moyer and Big Bill Haywood. The former sided with O'Neill, the latter with St. John. The breach between Moyer and Haywood never healed. It lasted through their imprisonment, their trial, and for the rest of their lives.

The controversy raging in the WFM brought on an act of violence. During the heat of an argument, a miner named Paddy Mulloney, a leader of the anti-Wobbly group, of the WFM, shot The Saint and permanently crippled him in the left hand.

4

THE MOYER-PETTIBONE-HAYWOOD CASE

THE INTERNAL TROUBLES of the WFM had its roots in differences other than the union's affiliation with the IWW. Radical and moderate leaders disagreed sharply over the question of raising funds to defend Moyer, Pettibone, and Haywood. This issue caused deep bitterness. The moderates resented giving money to aid men they considered to be troublemakers. As one moderate leader stated, "In my opinion, those three birds wouldn't hesitate to commit murder. . . . For all I know, they're guilty as sin! I hate to throw away our hard-earned dough to save the likes of them!"

However, the issue went beyond the personalities and characters of the three defendants. Some observers saw the impending trial as a critical time for the labor movement. "If they can pin this rap on Big Bill and the others, the bosses will go after every union man," an AFL official said. "And, believe me, I personally don't care what happens to Big Bill and his pals. It's not them. It's the labor movement that's at stake!"

Debate about the merits of the Moyer-Pettibone-Haywood case became purely academic on May 9, 1907, when the trial started in a Boise, Idaho, court before Judge Fremont Wood. The stuffy room was packed with spectators and newsmen, gasping in a May heat wave.

The trial aroused partisan feelings from coast to coast; few Americans failed to have some opinion about it. The Boise hearings were passionately stressed in the left-wing press. The general public was so interested in the trial that the Socialist newspaper, *The Appeal to Reason,* sold out a special edition of three million copies. Eugene Debs was featured in the paper with a signed front-page editorial entitled "Arouse Ye Slaves," which called upon the masses to "break down the prison bars that encage the incarcerated working-class martyrs."

Frank Heslewood crossed into Canada, where he recruited several hundred armed men for a march on Boise to liberate the prisoners. He gave up this wild scheme only after Frank Bohn, an IWW organizer, argued that the time was not yet right to start the "social revolution."

Although putting out every effort for his clients, Clarence Darrow was not happy with the role he was expected to play in the trial. "I wanted no part of a revolutionary crusade," the noted lawyer said. "Instead of permitting me to function as an attorney, the radicals felt I should be raising the red flag over the barricades."

Although he was a socialist, Darrow wanted to run the case along strictly legalistic lines with no political philosophies involved. He argued that nothing could be gained by injecting socialistic principles into the courtroom proceedings. "Neither judge nor jury care anything about the teachings of Karl Marx," he said.

Darrow even insisted that Debs should not cover the trial for *The Appeal to Reason.* Big Bill Haywood commented tartly that Darrow did not want Debs in court because "the mouthpiece wants to hog the limelight. . . ."

Relations between Haywood and Darrow were strained. The lawyer disliked Big Bill and made no attempt to hide his feelings. But this did not stop Darrow from believing in Haywood's innocence or conducting a magnificent defense on his behalf.

Darrow's strategy was to defend Haywood first on the assumption that by winning an acquittal for him, the case against Moyer and Pettibone would collapse. As the nation watched, the Boise trial got under way. It took several days to select a jury and then the lawyers got down to work.

William E. Borah, the junior senator from Idaho, headed the prosecution. Borah, a top-notch lawyer, would later be numbered among the country's foremost legislators. Handsome and silver-tongued, he made good newspaper copy with his mane of black hair and classic features. However, the imposing senator was outclassed by Darrow.

Borah's case rested upon a flimsy foundation that Darrow skillfully demolished by tearing apart McParlan's testimony and shattering Orchard's story. Darrow called an impressive array of witnesses in Haywood's behalf and proved beyond question that Big Bill never had any contact with Orchard and was almost a thousand miles away when Steunenberg died.

While discrediting Borah's star witnesses, Darrow also reminded the jury that the prosecuting attorney, along with Steunenberg and several others, recently had been indicted for illegal speculation in public timberland. Borah and his colleagues had been acquitted, but the unhappy incident weakened the impression the junior senator made on the jurors.

After being charged by Judge Wood, the jury stayed out for a long time. When it returned to the court, each man showed the strain of the wearying hours of deliberation. The verdict justified Darrow's strategy. The foreman announced "Not guilty!" and a ragged cheer went up from Wobbly sympathizers in the court.

On the basis of the Haywood verdict, Moyer and Pettibone were freed without trial. Harry Orchard, branded by his own confession, was sentenced to life imprisonment for the Steunenberg murder.

The acquittal of Haywood, so enthusiastically received in labor circles, brought an opposite reaction from the Mine Owners' Association, which issued a vitriolic statement denouncing the verdict. Judge Fremont Wood also revealed that the outcome of the trial displeased him. When sentencing Orchard, he expressed the belief that Haywood and the others were just as guilty.

Although Wobblies celebrated the courtroom triumph, it was a costly victory. The outcome of the trial enabled the moderate element in the WFM to get the upper hand and lead that militant union out of the IWW.

At the same time, the executive board of the WFM fired Haywood, who had emerged from the Boise trial as a popular labor hero with wide national appeal. So well known was Big Bill that theatrical managers plied him with offers to lecture on his experiences in prison and out.

But Big Bill's rise to prominence neither forged unity nor replenished the IWW treasury, which had been depleted in his defense. The trial exacted a crippling toll in money, energy, and personal relationships. After having been friends for years, Haywood and Moyer now were enemies.

If the Idaho ordeal made a moderate of Moyer, it set Haywood on an even more radical path. Clarence Darrow, a good friend of trade unions, was concerned about the future of the labor movement when he urged Haywood to "go back into the hills" and become a rancher again before he wrecked what had taken so long to build.

Big Bill Haywood rejected this advice; he seemed incapable of accepting advice from anyone. In the opinion of an associate, "Prison turned Big Bill into a wild man." He was in constant trouble while awaiting trial and made matters difficult for himself, his comrades, and the authorities. His rebellious behavior brought reprisals by the guards upon fellow prisoners. Once Moyer pleaded with him to calm down. "George and I can't take much more," he complained. "If you're so all-fired burned up, put an ice pack on your head!"

"Why don't you get it out from under your feet first?" snapped Big Bill.

His stay in prison soured Moyer on direct action as a union tactic. He now regarded it as "folly." A family man, Moyer wanted to avoid another term in jail, and his outlook became increasingly conservative.

Haywood, on the contrary, evolved into even more of a maverick. He frowned on what he termed "chicken-hearted policies" and talked constantly of sabotage, revolution, and class struggle, regarding as an enemy anyone whose opinion differed from his. Although Darrow had won the case, Haywood was hostile to the lawyer. A year after the trial, when George Pettibone died, Big Bill did not even attend his funeral. People meant nothing to him.

He grew so estranged from his once beloved wife, Jane, that he failed to attend her funeral ten years later. Mrs. Haywood, long an invalid, had embraced faith healing as a desperate measure to regain her health. Big Bill neither understood nor sympathized with his wife. He simply drifted away from her and his three daughters. For a time, he drank heavily, but quit when he realized that his habit was giving the IWW a bad name.

"Big Bill Haywood was not a lovable man," an associate said. "He treated his family badly and was hard to get along with. But no man, not even his worst enemies, could claim he ever was untrue to the IWW. All the feelings and sensibilities he had were poured into the movement. . . ."

When Haywood was expelled from the Western Federation of Miners, Vincent St. John, possibly Big Bill's only close friend, resigned from the union's executive board and devoted his full time to the IWW. The two men pooled their considerable organizing talents to save the IWW from collapse.

The Saint blamed the unhappy situation in the IWW on Daniel De Leon's political ambitions. In a magazine article on the Wobblies, St. John wrote:

> The first year was one of internal struggle for control by those who favored direct action and those who advocated political action. The two camps of socialist politicians looked upon the IWW as a battle ground on which to settle their respective merits and demerits. The labor fakers strove to fasten themselves upon the organization that they might continue to exist if the union was a success.

Haywood and St. John made ready for a finish fight with De Leon. They knew how much ill-feeling in the IWW he had fomented and were also aware that the bindle stiffs mistrusted both him and the Socialist Labor Party. They decided to force De Leon and his followers out of the IWW.

ONE BIG UNION

THE 1908 IWW CONVENTION, the fourth in its brief history, convened on October 1, in a ramshackle Chicago hall. Only twenty-six delegates were present for this meeting—a far cry from the two hundred in 1905. The small number indicated how far the IWW had slipped since then.

These delegates were a breed far different from the mixed bag of the founding congress. This time, only hard-core believers in industrial unions turned up.

Despite organizational upsets and upheavals, the idea of One Big Union spread from Maine to Washington State. Wobbly-inspired strikes erupted among loggers, miners, window washers, paper-mill workers, and streetcar railwaymen.

In December, 1906, even before the Boise trial, the IWW had carried out the first sitdown strike ever held in America, at the Schenectady, New York, plant of the General Electric Company.

In the period just prior to the 1908 convention, the IWW conducted many more labor struggles. For an organization that many "experts" had pronounced dead, the IWW was an astonishingly lively corpse.

The convention drew a colorful audience. Jack Walsh, a socialist turned Wobbly, led twenty bindle stiffs to Chicago. Sawmill workers, loggers, and migratory farmhands, these rugged men made their way to the Windy City riding freight trains, camping in hobo jungles, heating cans of "mulligan stew" over cook fires, and singing Wobbly songs. Walsh's bunch marched into the convention hall wearing blue-denim overalls, black shirts, red bandanas, and heavy work shoes known as "boondockers." En route to Chicago, they held IWW meetings, selling pamphlets and Wobbly songbooks to help defray expenses.

This self-styled "Overalls Brigade" was outspokenly opposed to De Leon, who sneered at them as the "bummery element" because they had "bummed" rides on freight trains. They reveled in this label and responded by singing, "Hallelujah I'm a Bum" to the tune of an old hymn, "Revive Us Again!" One verse of the song ran:

O, why don't you work
Like other men do?
How in hell can I work
When there's no work to do?

And then went into the rousing chorus:

Hallelujah I'm a bum,
Hallelujah bum again,
Hallelujah give us a handout,
To revive us again!

De Leon described Walsh's followers as "a detrimental force in the labor movement . . . who wanted to make the IWW a purely physical body without any intellectual basis. . . . Like bums and tramps, they slept on Chicago park benches along the Lake front and received from Walsh a stipend of thirty cents a day. . . ." On the other hand, the unkempt men of the "Overalls Brigade" regarded themselves as "genuine" rebels, "true sons of the working class."

(Interestingly, though these men adopted "Hallelujah I'm a Bum" as their theme song, they actually were "hoboes," not "bums" or "tramps." The difference among these itinerant categories was explained by one social historian: "The hobo works and wanders, the tramp dreams and wanders, the bum drinks and wanders. . . ." The word "hobo" probably originated from the British "hoe boy," or migratory farm worker. The migrants had colorful words to describe their varied seasonal occupations: "snipes" and "jerries" laid railroad sections; "splinter bellies" did rough carpentry work; "pearl divers" washed dishes; "sewer hogs" dug ditches; "timber" wolves felled trees; "gandy dancers" tamped ties on railroads and worked with "banjos," "mucksticks," or "anchors"—respectively, short-handled shovels, long-handled shovels, and tamping sticks.)

When Big Bill and The Saint arrived in Chicago, they were accompanied by a large group of adherents from Seattle, Spokane, Portland, Los Angeles, and San Francisco. These men were not delegates to the convention, but "observers" and "spectators." Most had belonged to the WFM, but, being firm believers in industrial unionism, quit that body when the miners union left the IWW. Although they had no vote on convention decisions, they gave loud vocal support to the Haywood-St. John faction and shouted down speakers in favor of De Leon.

There was one woman among the twenty-six accredited delegates, a teen-ager from New York named Elizabeth Gurley Flynn. At nineteen, she already had won recognition as a fiery militant. Miss Flynn, a dark-haired beauty, was descended from generations of Irish rebels. On her mother's side of the family she boasted kinship with George Bernard Shaw.

(During her years with the IWW, Elizabeth Gurley Flynn

was hailed as the "Joan of Arc of the Working Class" and "The Red Flame." The Wobbly songwriter, Joe Hill, used her as the inspiration for one of his best-known tunes, "The Rebel Girl.")

If past IWW conventions had been stormy, they were mild in comparison to the 1908 conclave. After electing Vincent St. John as permanent chairman, the delegates turned on De Leon, whom they irreverently dubbed "The Pope," for his pontifical manner.

No sooner had The Saint called the meeting to order than a resolution was made to expel De Leon on the grounds that he did not "work for wages." In accordance with the IWW constitution, this rendered him ineligible for membership. Another charge was that De Leon's credentials as a delegate were unacceptable because he had come to the convention as the representative of the Store and Office Workers Union. Actually, his foes claimed, he had no business in that organization, but should have joined the Printing and Publishing Union, since he edited a newspaper called *The People.*

When De Leon rose in rebuttal, hecklers shouted, "Sit down, Pope!" Ignoring them, De Leon proceeded to deliver a spirited defense of his position and his policies. However, he failed to impress the crowd. "He spoke on such a lofty plane that hardly anybody there understood his arguments," a delegate recalled.

Sometime after the convention, De Leon published the speech under the title, *The Intellectual Against the Worker,* which described exactly how he regarded himself. The gulf between the leader of the SLP and the Overalls Brigade could not be bridged. He did not comprehend the realities facing the bindle stiffs, but saw their plight as an exercise for his intellect. He propounded vague philosophical concepts and theories. To him the revolution presented a problem in semantics.

De Leon had no friends among the jerries, snipes, splinter bellies, timber wolves, gandy dancers, and pearl divers of the American working class. Although he posed as a spokesman of the working people, De Leon actually was the voice of the middle-class intellectuals and "parlor pinks."

The hostility manifested toward De Leon stemmed from the ideological differences that raged within the IWW. "Birth pains," one historian called them. "Infantile disorders," another observer said. At any rate, the brief honeymoon period between De Leon and the direct-action bloc was at an end. The delegates quarreled and wrangled for several days, finally refusing to seat De Leon.

However, Haywood and St. John wanted still more; they pressed to erase all vestiges of the Socialist Labor Party from the IWW. The "political" clause of the constitution's preamble was eliminated. From its beginnings the IWW had flirted with politics and politicians but was now returning to its original antipolitical concepts of industrial unionism.

"We learned the hard way that every politician was beating his own drum and playing his own game for his own purposes. We'd long recognized that the Republican and Democratic parties served the bosses. Next we had to realize that there also were labor fakers in the SLP," an IWW member stated sometime later.

(After his expulsion from the Chicago convention, De Leon took a handful of followers and founded his own IWW in Detroit. It existed merely to disseminate the gospel of industrial unionism according to Daniel De Leon. The Detroit IWW never made much headway and vanished altogether a few years after De Leon's death in 1914 at the age of sixty-two.)

With direct actionists finally in charge, the IWW came of age as a fighting labor organization. Although it could muster only five thousand dues-paying members after the 1908 convention, the Wobblies never had been in better shape. For the first time they were a cohesive force, firmly united in purpose and principle, loyal only to the One Big Union, unhampered by any political party.

Nearly every card-carrying Wobbly was a veteran of the picket lines. Rebels and radicals to the man, they intended to make the IWW the instrument for bringing a new social order to America. They pledged themselves to this goal with a vigor and courage that revamped the American labor movement and left an indelible imprint on the nation's soul.

THE GOLDFIELD STRIKE

DESPITE INNER weaknesses, the IWW had begun to make inroads on the labor front even before the 1908 convention. But the Wobblies met with only limited success in many of their endeavors, and some were outright failures. Most IWW-led strikes brought the workers only minor gains, and a few of the local unions formed by the Wobblies were stillborn.

Too often they wasted time, money, and strength on trivial organizational efforts. Big Bill Haywood was personally responsible for creating one of the most unlikely unions ever formed, the Bronco Busters and Range Riders Union, with a membership consisting of cowboys, a breed for whom Big Bill always had a soft spot. Late in 1905, when a traveling rodeo came to Denver, the Wobbly leader felt obliged to help the performers get higher pay. He persuaded Harry Brennan, a rodeo champion, to sign up the other men.

With Brennan as president and Tom Minor (Haywood's father-in-law) as secretary, the Bronco Busters and Range

Riders Union enrolled every rodeo performer in Denver. Before long, the BBRRU won the then extraordinary wage of $5.00 per day for broncobusters in rodeo season and a minimum of $50 per month for work on range and ranch.

However, the free and easy cowboys were not interested in unionization. When the average cowpoke came to town, he preferred whiskey, poker, and dance-hall girls to union meetings. Before many months had passed, the BBRRU died of apathy and vanished on the last roundup.

A splendid opportunity opened for the IWW while it was still suffering the pangs of its "infantile disorders." In 1905, Goldfield, Nevada, was enjoying the peak of a gold-rush boom. More than 30,000 people populated the town, the center for many gold-mining camps and prospectors. The Wobblies decided to use Goldfield as a pilot project in all-out industrial unionism.

Various trade unions had come there before the IWW; the WFM made good progress in Goldfield, while carpenters, printers, and other skilled workers were signed up by AFL unions. However, as was the case everywhere in the United States, Goldfield's unskilled workers belonged to no union at all. The IWW leaders decided to change that situation.

"We proceeded without force, without intimidation . . . to organize all wage workers in the community. . . . We gathered miners, clerks, stenographers, teamsters, dish washers, waiters, and other 'common' laborers into one big union —Local 77 of the IWW," a Wobbly organizer recalled.

Local 77 soon merged with Local 220 of the WFM and Goldfield's One Big Union became still bigger. Soon, there was a rush to join the Wobbly local. Even the newsboys of Goldfield joined the union. By the end of 1907, the IWW-WFM had signed up almost "every working stiff in sight," according to Vincent St. John, who led the IWW drive.

However, this Wobbly push created grave problems. In the summer of 1908, AFL carpenters were building a boxing arena in Goldfield, which had been selected as the site of the Joe Gans-Battling Nelson world lightweight championship bout. The carpenters firmly resisted the Wobblies; they rejected all attempts to recruit them into One Big Union. "I guess what got us mad was to be linked with pearl divers and such. We were craftsmen and proud of it," an AFL carpenter observed.

Vicious strife broke out in Goldfield between AFL and IWW men; blood was spilled on both sides. Tony Silva, an AFL official who owned a restaurant, attacked a Wobbly organizer, M. R. Preston, who was picketing the eating place in support of Silva's waitresses. They had joined the IWW and were striking for higher pay. Silva, incensed at the sight of a picket outside his restaurant, got into a violent argument with Preston. Words led to blows and Preston knocked Silva down. The restaurant owner drew a revolver, but Preston pulled his own gun and fatally wounded Silva. (At that time, there was nothing uncommon about carrying a pistol, especially in the West.)

A jury of Goldfield businessmen found Preston guilty of second-degree murder and sentenced him to a twenty-five-year prison term. After he had served seven years, a parole board released him on the grounds that he had killed Silva in self-defense.

"I've put in all this time behind bars only because I belonged to the IWW," Preston declared. "Had I shot a Wobbly in cold blood, that same jury would've given me a medal!"

Despite setbacks, the IWW won its spurs in Goldfield. The Wobblies established a $5.00 daily minimum wage for miners, a high level for that time. Under the IWW, not only miners, but also hotel employees, bartenders, restaurant workers, and store clerks enjoyed pay rises and better working conditions. Possibly the biggest beneficiaries of industrial unionism were railroad workers in the Goldfield region. The

IWW brought up their salaries from $1.75 for a ten-hour day to $4.50 for an eight-hour one.

Even as Wobbly stock was soaring, Nevada authorities, led by Governor John Sparks and the Mine Owners Association, took steps to crush the IWW in Goldfield. The Nevada legislature passed an act creating a special state militia that could be used by the governor to suppress "civil disorders."

The IWW, according to a Wobbly leaflet, protested the formation of "legalized uniformed murderers . . . under the disguise of state militia. . . . We know full well that such a force will be used against the working class."

As Sparks was recruiting his militia, the Mine Owners Association announced an open-shop policy. This meant that mine operators flatly refused to deal with any union and could ask for the militia to keep union organizers away from the mines.

Raising the cry that "law and order must be maintained," Sparks rushed troops to Goldfield. Bayonets ruled the streets and crippled the IWW organizing campaign.

But it took a blow more crushing than the militia to drive the IWW out of Goldfield. In late 1907, a financial panic swept the United States, bringing on an economic depression that became fully effective in 1908. As business dwindled and unemployment soared, the Goldfield boom burst like a pricked balloon. The once-thriving place became a ghost town.

IWW locals were wiped out, not only in Goldfield, but in all parts of the United States as well, when their members were forced into what one journalist described as "the wretched army of the unemployed."

In a pessimistic mood, Vincent St. John wrote: "Our locals are dissolving by the dozens . . . during this awful period . . . and the general headquarters at Chicago is maintained only by terrific sacrifice and determination."

Despite disappointment and ultimate failure in Goldfield,

The Saint regarded the Nevada experience as a high point of IWW history. In 1917, he noted:

> Under the IWW sway in Goldfield . . . the minimum wage for all kinds of labor was $4.50 a day and the eight hour day was universal. The highest point of efficiency for any labor organization was reached by the IWW in Goldfield. . . . No committee was ever sent to any employers. The unions adopted wage scales and regulated hours. The secretary posted the same on a bulletin board outside the union hall and it was the LAW. . . . The employers were forced to come and see the committee.

Although times were hard and the immediate outlook bleak as the depression widened, the Wobblies were optimistic about the future. They had not lost the vision of Ralph Chaplin's "glowing dream," and still hopefully sang:

> When our cause is all triumphant
> And we claim our Mother Earth,
> And the nightmare of the present fades away,
> We shall live with love and laughter,
> We, who now are little worth,
> And we'll not regret the price we have to pay.

7

TROUBLE, FROM McKEES ROCKS TO THE MESABI

THE FATE OF industrial unions in America seemed dubious in the face of depression, the collapse of the Goldfield local, and the defection of the WFM. The movement revived a bit during the 1908 presidential election campaign, when Eugene Debs was the Socialist Party's candidate.

Debs made a cross-country tour aboard a train known as the "Red Special"; in his speeches, he stressed the benefits of industrial unionism. Although they usually spurned politics, Wobblies flocked to hear Debs and to serenade him with IWW songs when he spoke from the rear platform of the Red Special.

Those who predicted the end of the IWW proved to be false prophets. On June 28, 1909, the Wobblies roared back to life as the result of a spontaneous strike in McKees Rocks, Pennsylvania, a Pittsburgh suburb. The dispute flared in the workshops of the Pressed Steel Car Company, a subsidiary of the United States Steel Corporation. Pressed Steel Car completely dominated McKees Rocks. Most of its population, nearly all foreign-born, worked for the company, traded at company-run stores, and lived in company-owned houses.

That June day, the management of Pressed Steel Car announced a new method of wage payment, known as the pool system. This meant that a foreman would receive all the pay for his section and then distribute it to the workers according to the amount of work each had turned out.

Although they were unorganized, the workers objected to the plan and walked off the job. These greenhorns, only recently arrived in the United States from Germany, Italy, and Russia, spoke little English, were strange to American ways, but knew a lot about trade unionism. The Russians had fled their native country after taking part in the unsuccessful 1905 revolution against the czar. The Germans had been militant unionists back home, as had the Italians. (In addition to these nationalities, Pressed Steel Car workers also included Hungarians, Poles, Slovaks, Irish, Bulgarians, and Greeks.)

At first the Pressed Steel Car strikers appealed to the AFL Machinists Union, which had organized the skilled workers employed by the company, but that group was not interested in the unskilled foreigners. Some strikers had heard of the IWW and got in touch with William Trautmann, who hurried to McKees Rocks with a team of Wobbly organizers.

The company responded by turning McKees Rocks into an armed camp. Special deputies were hired and armed with clubs and guns to supplement several hundred mounted state police against the six thousand resolute strikers.

Violence broke out almost at once. A striker named Steve Horvath was killed in a clash with company guards recruited from Pittsburgh's underworld. Thousands of strikers representing fifteen nationalities attended the funeral.

The Pennsylvania Constabulary—mounted state troopers—brutally attacked strike meetings and picket lines, mercilessly clubbing men, women, and even children. Within a few days more than one hundred people had been hurt, many of them seriously. The police were particularly savage, dragging arrested strikers off to jail behind horses. Small wonder that Russian-born strikers dubbed the troopers "Cossacks."

Outraged by this cruel treatment, the strikers hit back. A group calling itself "The Unknown Committee" warned the Constabulary that a trooper would pay "in blood" for every striker killed or wounded. They made good this threat when Cossacks charged a peaceful union meeting touching off a gun battle in which three troopers and four strikers were killed. This bloodshed ended the violence. As William Trautmann noted: "The chief of the Cossacks called off his bloodhounds. After that shooting, no striker, deputy or trooper was hurt. Organized and disciplined physical force . . . stopped the wanton destruction of life at McKees Rocks."

Once the strikers were able to maintain mass picket lines without interference, the directors of Pressed Steel Car, realizing that public sentiment was on the side of the strikers, capitulated to the union. The old wage system was restored and several other grievances settled favorably for the workers. The Wobblies had not only won a major victory, but also gained the confidence of immigrant workers in the East. Rebuffed by the AFL, they had found a champion and protector in the IWW.

Workers began flocking to join the Wobblies, both in the East and the West. Lumberjacks in Montana and California struck and won under the IWW banner. So did metalworkers in Pennsylvania and farm laborers in Washington State. The IWW was enjoying a lusty rebirth.

Much credit for the IWW's revival was due the fearless young organizers who sparked the fight for industrial unionism. One of the most effective and outstanding Wobbly leaders was twenty-four-year-old Joe Ettor, who guided the

IWW campaign among East Coast immigrant workers. Brooklyn-born Ettor was fluent in Italian, Polish, Hungarian, and Yiddish. He could reach workers in their own tongues. A short, stocky Italian, with a thick shock of black hair upon which a small hat sat jauntily, Ettor always wore a flannel shirt and a flowing bow tie. He had a kindly, boyish face, unlimited physical vitality, and a strong resonant voice.

"When Joe Ettor spoke," an observer remembered, "everyone listened. Workers loved him. He was their idol."

Between 1908 and 1916 Ettor led numerous labor struggles. During those eight years he organized shoe workers in Brooklyn; textile workers in Lawrence, Massachusetts; Western Union messengers in New York City; and metal miners on the Mesabi Range in Minnesota.

During the Mesabi Range strike of 1916, Ettor disobeyed certain directives of the GEB. For this, he was expelled from the IWW and took no further part in the labor movement. When he died in 1948 at the age of sixty-two, the once fiery Wobbly was peacefully and prosperously running a fruit orchard in San Clemente, California.

But between 1908 and 1916 there was little tranquillity for Joe Ettor or any other active Wobbly. From 1909 to 1912 the IWW concentrated its major organizing efforts among the migratory workers of the West Coast—the underpaid, mistreated bindle stiffs. Drifting from job to job, they were victimized by unscrupulous employment "sharks," who ran job agencies in the West Coast cities where bindle stiffs came to search for work.

Acting as hiring agents for employers, the sharks charged migratory workers a fee for locating a job. This would not have been so bad, but the sharks made deals for foremen on farms, in logging and construction camps, on road gangs, and in mines that used bindle stiffs, to ensure a big turnover of workers. The available jobs always had "one gang coming, one gang working, and one gang leaving," according to an observer.

The more rapidly men were hired and fired, the more fees there were for sharks to split with the foremen who did the hiring and the firing. Often, as many as five men would pay a shark for the same job, only to be unemployed again within a few hours.

"Foremen were more interested in getting their cut of the shark's fees than to have a job properly filled and the work efficiently done," an old-time Wobbly remembered.

IWW organizers urged the bindle stiffs to boycott the sharks, thus forcing employers to hire workers directly or to set up honest employment agencies.

When Wobbly speakers climbed on soapboxes to address crowds of migratory workers, the sharks, many of whom were local political hacks, tried to silence the "agitators." Police often cooperated with the sharks and many Wobblies were arrested. In order to end this abuse, the IWW undertook actions that became known as "free-speech fights."

The Wobblies had several reasons for launching such campaigns. The constitutional right of freedom of speech was at stake. Free-speech fights often captured newspaper headlines, thus giving the Wobblies a chance to expose the awful conditions under which bindle stiffs lived and worked.

When the free-speech fights began in the early part of 1909, some 3,500,000 of the 10,250,000 unskilled workers in the United States were migratories moving from one seasonal job to another. On the West Coast, they made up most of the labor force.

The food and quarters provided for them by employers were appalling. Red Doran, a Wobbly organizer, described how bindle stiffs lived:

> Camps were unsanitary, abominable places. . . . The food was of the poorest quality and dished out in a slovenly manner . . . on rusty, battered tinware. The men slept in

> crude bunkhouses with double-bunk beds that were infested with bedbugs and lice. . . . There were no washhouses . . . a single pump served fifteen or twenty men.

The nomadic bindle stiffs were defenseless against such exploitation; economically weak, they were without resources or influence. No one cared about these wanderers until the Wobblies came along and sought to change their lot.

8 THE FREE-SPEECH BATTLES

"WE'RE GOING TO YANK the sharks off the back of the working class!" an IWW street-corner orator told a crowd of lumberjacks in Missoula, Montana. "If we stick together we can do it easily!"

Such Wobbly tirades against the employment sharks of Missoula began having an effect. The sharks found it difficult to round up men for jobs as the bindle stiffs, taking IWW advice, found work through other avenues. The Missoula employment agents were losing money, as were the foremen whose share of the take was dwindling away.

Claiming that the Wobblies were seditious, unpatriotic, and a menace to the community, the sharks induced the Missoula city council to pass an ordinance banning IWW-sponsored street meetings. The Wobblies met the challenge head on. A call went out from IWW organizers in Missoula for "footloose rebels . . . to come at once and defend the Bill of Rights!" In response to this summons, Wobblies from all over the West hitched, rode freights, and hiked to

Missoula. They poured in by the scores and asserted their right to free speech on every street corner in Missoula. Young men and women mounted soapboxes to read aloud the Declaration of Independence, recite Lincoln's Gettysburg Address or even the Lord's Prayer.

As soon as he started to talk, a speaker was arrested. The city jail filled up quickly with Wobblies singing "Hallelujah I'm a Bum!" and "Solidarity Forever!" No matter how many were arrested and jailed, others came to take their places on the speakers' platforms.

After ten unrelenting days of this action, the harassed city officials rescinded the anti-IWW edict. Missoula simply could not afford to keep feeding prisoners and paying extra police. Besides, the free-speech fight was ruining business in Missoula. Shoppers, afraid to get involved, stayed away from town. Nor was the city council happy about the unfavorable national publicity arising from the issue. It was far easier and wiser to repeal the ordinance than to try enforcing a repressive law.

Missoula was only the first of some thirty free-speech battles fought by the IWW in less than a decade. Not all of them were such cut-and-dried victories for the Wobblies. Some towns and cities put up bitter resistance to the IWW free-speech crusaders. Missoula was a pushover compared to the struggle that took place in Spokane, Washington. That city, the hub of a region rich in agriculture, mining, and lumbering, was a center for hiring out migratory workers. Spokane's employment sharks were among the most ruthless in the West. To combat them, the IWW held "educational" meetings on Front Avenue, also known as Agency Row because so many employment offices were located there.

"Don't buy jobs!" the Wobblies urged the bindle stiffs. They pressed for an antiagency boycott and called upon employers to hire workmen through an IWW-run hiring hall that would set minimum wages, working conditions, and length of employment. This brought howls from sharks, foremen, and employers. Each stood to lose unless the Wobblies were silenced.

Agents and employers persuaded the Spokane city council to ban all street meetings after January 1, 1909. For some months, the IWW obeyed this injunction, since it applied to other groups as well. But when the law was amended so that the Salvation Army could hold street assemblies, the Wobblies kicked up a storm.

On October 28, 1909, an IWW member was arrested for "soapboxing," as street-corner speaking was called. The next day, *The Industrial Worker* ran an appeal headlined: "Wanted! Men to fill the Jails of Spokane!" This was followed by a letter to all IWW locals in the area: "November 2nd. Free Speech Day. Lovers of free speech are asked to be in Spokane on that date. . . . Our meetings must be orderly . . . no irregularities will be tolerated . . ."

Tuesday, November 2, 1909, saw the opening of a five-month-long defiance of the Spokane ban. That day, several thousand Wobblies marched from the IWW hall on Front Avenue to challenge the city officials. The first day, one speaker after another mounted a platform, but seldom got any further than to say, "Friends and fellow workers," before being yanked down by waiting police and tossed into jail for thirty days on disorderly-conduct charges. By midnight, 103 arrests had been made.

Among those taken was one Wobbly who never had made a speech in public until his turn came to get on the speakers' stand and subject himself to arrest. Shaking from stage fright, he blurted out, "Friends and fellow workers!" At the moment, there was no policeman around to collar him. He stood silently for a moment, incapable of uttering a word.

Finally he managed to wail, "Where the hell are the cops? What's taking them so long!"

By the end of November, some six hundred Wobblies had been jailed, with more coming in every day. They were herded into overcrowded cells, fed slops, and subjected to merciless beatings. When they protested this treatment, the police shut off all ventilation in the jail and turned on the steam heat until the cells became "airless furnaces," according to one prisoner.

An abandoned school lacking heating or bathing facilities was converted into a temporary prison to handle the overflow from the city jail. In addition, the U.S. government gave the city authorities permission to use crumbling Fort Wright in which to lock up arrested Wobblies.

Day after day, the IWW applied pressure. Gradually, public opinion outside Spokane swung to the Wobblies. The mass arrests, police brutality, and wretched treatment of the prisoners brought mounting sympathy for the free-speech fighters. So contagious was this feeling that it even infected residents of Spokane. One day it manifested itself in a public demonstration of support of the prisoners. When the Wobblies confined at the schoolhouse were marched under guard to the central police station for a much needed bath, crowds of Spokane citizens lined the way. The onlookers applauded the prisoners and bombarded them with sandwiches, packs of smoking tobacco, fruit, and cake.

Such displays, plus the rising costs of persecuting the Wobblies, the loss of business in Spokane, and the unsavory reputation the city was getting, finally convinced officials that it was more sensible to negotiate with the IWW and reach a settlement.

The Spokane Free Speech Fight came to an end on March 4, 1910, with almost total victory for the IWW. All prisoners went free, the right to speak in the streets was granted, nineteen of the worst employment sharks were forced to close shop. The surviving agencies operated legitimately, charging modest fees only when a job was assured under decent working conditions. However, the practice of direct hiring through the union hall eventually made employment agencies of that sort unnecessary.

A few months after Spokane, the Wobblies once again had a free-speech fight on their hands. This one was in Fresno, California, where IWW organizer Frank Little, a veteran of Missoula and Spokane, headed a local union of unskilled fruit pickers.

The trouble started during December, 1910, when a contractor, unable to hire men at the starvation wages he was paying, complained to the Fresno chief of police that Wobbly agitators were to blame for the labor shortage. "Those clowns are giving the men wrong ideas," he grumbled. "We ought to put the clamp on those I Won't Work troublemakers."

A Fresno newspaper, aroused that the Wobblies had "infiltrated" their fair city, called for a "whipping post and a cat-o'-nine-tails, well seasoned by being soaked in salt water," as the proper way to handle "loafers, bums, and anarchists."

The Fresno police opened a campaign of intimidation against the Wobblies. They raided IWW headquarters, broke up their outdoor meetings, and arrested Wobblies on vagrancy charges.

One of the first to be jailed was Frank Little, who served twenty-eight days in solitary confinement. As soon as he was out he telegraphed IWW headquarters in Chicago, asking for help.

Once more the call for "footloose rebels" went forth. The cry "Free Speech Fight!" echoed in camps, hobo jungles, and IWW meeting rooms. As in the past, the Wobblies responded, ready for battle. From Portland, Oregon, came two hundred bindle stiffs, who rode the rods to the California state line, where they quit the freight cars to avoid railway police.

They made the rest of the trek on foot, a hike of almost three hundred miles to Fresno. Part of the way, the men floundered through a blizzard in the Siskiyou Mountains. Another hundred Wobblies left St. Louis for California, 1,500 miles away. Reinforcements joined them on the march until the original band numbered a thousand when it came to Fresno. By early spring, 1911, more than five thousand IWWs were reported massing in Denver for the trip to Fresno.

The city's jail was jammed with singing, shouting rebels. The Wobblies gave their keepers a hard time; indeed many Wobblies believed that the function of the oppressed-in-jail is to give the oppressors difficulty. Wobblies in prison were not at all docile. Speakers, clinging to the bars of cell windows, harangued cheering crowds gathered in the street outside the prison. One day when the Wobbly orators refused an order to stop, the warden had fire hoses turned on the "agitators." Using mattresses as shields, the Wobblies continued their defiance until the cells were knee-deep in icy water.

The Fresno Free Speech Fight dragged on into March, 1911. At that time the City Fathers heard rumors of the Wobbly mobilization in Denver. The specter of five thousand militants converging on their city so terrified the Fresno authorities that on March 9, 1911, they repealed the speaking edict and freed all jailed Wobblies.

The prisoners were let out in small groups, an hour or so apart. Free-speech fighters went to IWW headquarters, gathered up their bindles, and trudged out of town to find work. They had been soldiers in a battle for the right to speak; now they were wayfarers again, far down at the bottom of the economic heap.

But they departed from Fresno with pride in their step, singing a verse that had been added to the favorite Wobbly refrain, "Hallelujah I'm a Bum":

> Springtime has come,
> And I'm out of jail
> Without any money,
> Without any bail!

THE SAN DIEGO STRUGGLE

AT ABOUT THE TIME the Wobblies were winning in Fresno, serious labor violence flared in Los Angeles. The building of the Los Angeles *Times* was bombed, with a loss of twenty-one lives. When this occurred, Los Angeles was in the throes of a general strike. The trade unions were trying to force the closed shop on the employers of the city. The *Times*, owned and edited by Harrison Gray Otis, a diehard foe of unionism, vehemently opposed the closed shop both in principle and in practice. "No American should be forced to join a union if he doesn't want to do so!" Otis ranted. "Those who try to push unionism on us are no better than traitors! They are not real Americans! They are the hirelings of foreign intriguers who intend to topple our government and destroy the American way of life!"

Day after day Otis-authored editorials of that sort appeared in the paper. When the bomb went off, hardly anyone in Los Angeles was surprised that the *Times* had been the target.

Police investigation of the tragedy led to the arrest of Joseph J. McNamara, secretary of the Structural Iron Workers Union, and his younger brother, James B. McNamara, a typographer who belonged to the Typographical Union. They were accused of the crime on the "confession" of one Ortie McManigal, who claimed to have participated in the deed, which he alleged the McNamaras had "masterminded." Although McManigal had an unsavory reputation, he told a story that was accepted by press and public without question or reservation.

Antiunion sentiment, always strong in California, reached an all-time high with the arrest of the McNamara brothers. Because the IWW backed them, the Wobblies received the backlash of reaction against unions. Passions were whipped up by the McNamara trial. Led by the IWW, militants called for a general strike as a step to free the "martyred brothers" and to smash the "frameup" against the two working-class "heroes."

When the McNamara case went to court, a free-speech fight was raging in San Diego, California. For once, the Wobblies were not fighting it alone. The San Diego situation had developed shortly after the Fresno affair came to a conclusion. Worried San Diego businessmen prevailed upon the mayor to outlaw street meetings in order to forestall "another Fresno."

The ban was to become effective on January 1, 1912. But before that date, opponents of the law, among whom were anarchists, socialists, single taxers, Wobblies, and some AFL locals, formed a Free Speech League, and vowed to "keep constitutional rights" in San Diego.

The official mood of the city was expressed in a San Diego *Tribune* editorial urging that free-speech demonstrators either be shot or hanged. "Such people," the *Tribune* declared, "are the waste materials of creation and should be drained off into the sewer of oblivion."

However, on January 1, 1912, more than five thousand men and women marched to protest the oppressive law. Hundreds of them were arrested and the bellicose *Tribune* roared: "Shoot them! Shoot them all! That would settle matters in an hour!"

The IWW rallied its forces for an all-out free-speech fight in San Diego. But as the San Diego struggle was shaping up, the Wobblies, their allies, indeed the entire labor movement, was dealt a stunning blow. The McNamaras pleaded guilty to the Los Angeles *Times* bombing. They did so on the advice of their attorney, Clarence Darrow, whom the Structural Iron Workers had hired to defend the brothers.

Darrow some years later wrote that because his clients were charged with first-degree murder and faced the death penalty if found guilty, and because he felt sentiment was running strongly against them, he had urged the McNamaras to plead guilty to a lesser charge and thus avoid the hangman.

The brothers initially refused to go along with him, but Darrow was persuasive and the prosecution agreed to cooperate by letting them off with comparatively light sentences. However, after Darrow had entered the guilty pleas in a tense, crowded courtroom, he realized that the trial judge, Cyrus F. McNutt, and John D. Fredericks, the state's attorney, had double-crossed him. Joseph McNamara received a fifteen-year sentence, while James was given life, instead of the few years that had been promised.

The conviction of the brothers unloosed an unprecedented terror against unions and radicals. The special victim was the IWW. Although the McNamaras never had belonged to the Wobblies, the public believed the opposite. Newspapers played up the IWW theory of "direct action." In the popular mind this was linked with dynamiting and bombing.

In San Diego, where the free-speech fight was still on, local businessmen, frustrated and angered over the failure of city authorities to crush the Wobblies, took matters into their own hands. Egged on by the *Tribune,* they formed anti-IWW vigilante groups and San Diego endured a nightmare of untrammeled brutality. Night riders dished out justice with whip, gun, and tar and feathers.

Wobblies who had served out jail terms were seized, beaten, thrown into autos, driven out of town, flogged, and warned to steer clear of San Diego. The superpatriotic vigilantes did not limit their savagery to the IWW. When the editor of the San Diego *Herald* came out in support of the free-speech fight, he was kidnapped by masked men and severely trounced. The vigilantes racked up a dismal record of sadistic bestiality. In one case, they whipped a man, rolled him in hot tar and feathers, and branded him on the back with the letters IWW.

Vigilantism grew to such an extent that Governor Hiram Johnson of California, no liberal and opposed to the Wobblies, declared that "private terrorism" had to be curbed.

Johnson sent a special investigator, Colonel Harris Weinstock, to San Diego. The colonel's report exposed the shocking tactics both of police and vigilantes. According to Weinstock, there was "much needless brutality on the part of police officers. . . ." IWW members and sympathizers had been "taken by force out of the city . . . and subjected to inhuman beatings by a body of men, some of whom were police officers . . . and some private citizens. . . ." Colonel Weinstock further called the governor's attention to the "passive resistance, the lack of violence and drunkenness among the protestors. . . . It is in startling contrast to the comportment of the self-styled vigilantes. . . ."

Johnson approved Weinstock's report and ordered state law officers into San Diego for the purpose of "curtailing and bringing to a conclusion . . . the rampant violence." With this intervention, San Diego gradually returned to normal.

During the summer of 1912, free-speech prisoners were released from jail and violence against the Wobblies diminished. By September, the IWW was holding outdoor meetings without interference. San Diego had come back to sanity from its temporary madness.

In the many free-speech fights that flared over the years, the worst took place in 1916. The Wobblies had been leading a free-speech fight in Everett, Washington, a port city on Puget Sound. The usual violence and bloodshed resulted as vigilantes attacked Wobblies without mercy. Men were beaten senseless and left on the city's garbage dump. IWW organizers were forced to run the gauntlet between ranks of drunken vigilantes and special deputies who swung at them with nail-studded baseball bats.

The tempo of violence increased daily.

A newspaperman wrote from Everett: "This city is living at a murderous pitch. Armed specials and vigilantes . . . swagger about like a conquering army. . . . I predict that something dreadful will happen here soon."

"Something dreadful" was the Everett Massacre, which occurred on November 5, 1916, when the free-speech fight was entering its sixth month.

About three hundred Wobblies set sail for Everett from Seattle across Puget Sound. They were making the trip in two small steamers, the *Verona* and the *Calista.* The *Verona* hauled anchor first, its decks crowded with singing Wobblies. "Hold the fort,/ For we are coming!/ Union men be strong!" they sang as the *Verona* approached Pier No. Two, on the Everett docks.

The passengers did not suspect that two hundred rifle-toting vigilantes and deputy sheriffs were lying in wait at the pier. As the *Verona* turned broadside, fusillades from shore swept the deck of the steamer. Men on the steamer fell dead and wounded; the singing turned to hoarse shouts of pain, fear, and anger as Wobblies scurried to take cover. The *Verona's* captain swung her around, remaining faithfully at his post while bullets shattered the pilothouse windows and splintered the bridge. The vigilante guns killed five IWWs and wounded thirty-one. Losses among the attackers ran to two dead and nineteen wounded.

The *Verona* fled toward Seattle, warning the *Calista* to return as well. When the vessels reached shore, Seattle police, alerted from Everett by telephone, were waiting on the dock. They arrested seventy-four Wobblies on charges of murdering the two vigilantes. (No one ever was arrested for the killing of the IWW men.)

With headlines shrieking "IWW Murderers!," the Everett Massacre made front pages all over the country. Washington State newspapers demanded the wholesale execution of the seventy-four Wobblies in the hands of the police.

The first man to be tried was Tom Tracy, the IWW leader in Washington. With a rare show of solidarity, AFL unions joined in Tracy's defense. A prominent West Coast attorney, George F. Vanderveer, headed a brilliant defense staff. Tracy's trial, which started in March, 1917, lasted until May. The prosecution sought to prove that Tracy had fired the first shot from the *Verona* and the vigilantes had acted only to protect themselves.

A parade of prosecution witnesses luridly described how the Wobblies had come in "pouring lead from the *Verona*," which one man swore was "bristling with guns." All who testified against Tracy vowed that he had been standing at the steamboat's bow, firing an automatic rifle.

When all the testimony was in, Vanderveer requested the court to order a reenactment of the November 5 tragedy. "This time, of course, without bloodshed," the defense attorney quipped.

The demonstration clearly proved that it was impossible

to recognize anyone on the *Verona* from shore at one hundred yards, or even fifty yards, without binoculars. Vanderveer had cleverly made prosecution witnesses admit during cross-examination that none had field glasses. He also showed that the casualties suffered by the vigilantes probably had come from their own men during the confusion on the pier when the shooting started. He further had wormed out of the witnesses that there had been "quite a bit of drinking" going on among the ambushers.

The case against Tracy was smashed. He and his seventy-three codefendants were acquitted. The Everett Massacre brought greater prestige to the IWW than it ever before had enjoyed. The men of the *Verona* had not given their lives in vain.

With Tracy's trial, the era of the free-speech fights came to an end. It had been an important phase in the struggle for democracy, clearly demonstrating the power of mass passive resistance. But this was a costly tactic that laid the IWW open to bloody reprisals. Long before the Everett Massacre, as far back as 1912, certain Wobbly leaders had argued that the IWW should throw its full strength into building industrial unions and not "squander men and money" in free-speech fights.

"We are rebels, revolutionaries and trade unionists, not publicity seekers," a Wobbly organizer declared. "The future of the working class lies in industrial unions and not the right to speak on street corners. . . . When the One Big Union takes power, workingmen will have all the free speech they want, although I can't guarantee the same for the bosses."

Thus, while free-speech fights still were carried on in the West after 1912, the main thrust of the IWW was centered in the East with its thousands of immigrant industrial workers. The time had come to "light the fires of revolt among the downtrodden and exploited laboring masses," according to an IWW leader.

The torch was aflame and the blaze caught in the textile mills of Lawrence, Massachusetts, where foreign-born men, women, and children toiled under near-slave conditions at what were properly termed "starvation wages."

THE LAWRENCE STRIKE I

IN DECEMBER, 1911, the average Lawrence textile worker put in fifty-six hours weekly at a rate of $.16 per hour, which gave him a wage of $8.96, if he had no time lost. (About 15,000 mill workers, mostly young boys and girls, received only $.12 per hour.)

Of the 85,000 people living in Lawrence, over 60,000 depended for a living on mill wages. Close to 40,000 persons—nearly everyone over the age of fourteen—worked for the American Woolen Company, which owned most of the local textile mills. (Lawrence, a major center of textile weaving, stood on the banks of the Merrimack River, one of a string of textile cities—Manchester and Nashua, in New Hampshire, and Lowell, Massachusetts.)

William N. Wood, the president of the American Woolen Company, was the son of a poor Portuguese fisherman from the Azores. As a young man, Wood had risen from poverty by marrying a wealthy girl. However, most of his immense fortune came from the textile empire he had created—the American Woolen Company, an amalgamate of thirty-four mills with a yearly output valued at $45,000,000. According to the standards of the day, this made the American Woolen Company one of the nation's industrial giants. If William Wood had become a multimillionaire from his textile plants, his workers earned scarcely enough to keep alive.

Even with an entire family working, making ends meet was an almost impossible task. Mill workers lived in wretched tenement flats that rented for weekly rates of $1.00 to $6.00. The houses were poorly built, frigid in winter, sweltering in summer; they crawled with roaches, bedbugs, and other vermin. There were no bathrooms; the kitchen sink served as a tub on Saturday nights. Toilets were outdoor privies.

(After a visit to Lawrence, a New York journalist wrote: "I've seen better living quarters in the most fetid slums of Europe than exist in Lawrence, Massachusetts.")

Bread was the staple diet for most millworkers, along with molasses and beans. Meat was so seldom served that its appearance on the table "brought shouts of joy from the children," according to an observer. Lawrence workers eked out a bitter existence.

In an article on working conditions prevailing in the textile industry, a national magazine commented: "One can not say that the workers are living. . . . Their joyless life is a treadmill of drudgery. Robbed of youth and childhood, they can only await the release of death."

Many, indeed, too many, of the workers found the "release of death." Dr. Elizabeth Shapleigh, a Lawrence physician, wrote: "A considerable number of boys and girls die within the first two or three years after starting work. . . . Thirty-six out of every 100 of all men and women who work in the mills die before reaching the age of 25." Malnutrition, work strain, and occupational diseases cut the lifespan of the average Lawrence worker twenty-two years shorter than that of other factory workers, according to Dr. Shapleigh.

Most Lawrence millworkers were either immigrants or the

children of immigrants. Few had been educated beyond grammar school; many left in the fourth or fifth grade, going into the mills even before the legal working age of fourteen.

Unions in Lawrence were weak and ineffectual. The IWW had founded a local there in 1907, but five years later, it could count only three hundred dues-paying members, all greenhorns who barely could speak or even understand English.

Skilled, English-speaking workers were organized in three craft locals of the AFL United Textile Workers Union (UTW). Once, 2,500 workers had been enrolled in these groups, but their membership had dwindled to about two hundred.

In thirty years, Lawrence workers had gone out on strike three times—1882, 1894, and 1902—but each walkout had been crushed by troops, thugs, and scabs (strikebreakers).

The memorable 1912 strike was triggered by an act of the Massachusetts state legislature that supposedly benefited the workers. Responding to rising public feeling over the bad conditions in the textile mills, the legislators passed a law reducing the work week from fifty-six hours to fifty-four, for women and children. The ordinance was to become effective on January 1, 1912. Millworkers feared that the company would take advantage of the situation and cut their pay by two hours.

After January 1, it became apparent that their misgivings were justified. The mills speeded up machines so that fifty-six hours' work could be done in a shorter period and announced that henceforth the maximum work week would be fifty-four hours for every employee—man, woman, or child.

The IWW local immediately wrote President Wood asking if wages would be affected by this edict. There was no reply and the workers grew restive. If pay was reduced by two hours, the workers would be losing $.32, the price of three loaves of bread.

The pay period after New Year's Day came on January 11. A group of Polish women workers were the first to be paid; immediately they noticed that their envelopes were short by $.32. Resentment flared into action. "Short pay! Short pay!" the women screamed. Shutting down the machines, the angry workers poured out into the street, where they were joined by hundreds of other workers—men and women—yelling, cursing, shaking fists, and raising the same desperate cry, "Short pay!"

As the work stoppage spread, all Lawrence boiled. The Wobblies jumped into the affair, issuing a leaflet in a half-dozen languages, calling for a general textile strike under the slogan, "Better to starve fighting, than to starve working!" Within twenty-four hours, not a loom turned in Lawrence, "The unbelievable has happened," a Lawrence merchant noted in his diary. "The greenhorns have risen!"

The organizer of the IWW local quickly realized that the situation was too much for him to handle alone. Hundreds of workers were flocking to him, begging for leadership and guidance. He sent a telegram to Joe Ettor in New York City, begging him to help. Ettor needed no second summons. He arrived in Lawrence on the night train, accompanied by another fiery Wobbly organizer, twenty-seven-year-old, Italian-born Arturo Giovannitti, a rabble-rousing orator and poet who edited an Italian radical newspaper, *Il Proletario* (*The Worker*).

Ettor soon whipped the strike into shape. A committee comprised of two members from each nationality group was formed. This board ran the strike. Under Ettor's guidance, the committee formulated a list of demands that included a fifteen-percent increase in wages for a fifty-four-hour week, double pay for overtime, and no reprisals against workers participating in the strike.

These demands, translated into many languages, were printed on leaflets and circulated all over town. When the mayor of Lawrence read the leaflet, he told an aide: "So that's the way it is, eh? I'll teach the bohunks a lesson they'll never forget!" (In the slang of the day, any immigrant from southern and eastern Europe was called a "bohunk.")

The mayor called out a company of city militia and soon the streets were patrolled by squads with bayonets fixed on loaded rifles. The Lawrence Establishment had accepted the challenge of the workers. From its onset, the strike was no ordinary labor dispute. One historian called it, "A social revolution in miniature. . . . On the one hand were the entrenched interests, the mill owners and their tools who held political office . . . on the other, were the workers, struggling to rise out of the depths."

Elizabeth Gurley Flynn and a veteran Wobbly, Jim Thompson, came to assist Ettor and Giovannitti. The dynamic Wobbly leaders headed mass picket lines that tangled with police, militia, and company guards. Before the strike was even a few days old, many pickets had been injured or arrested.

Once the first burst of enthusiasm waned, the strikers began to grow uneasy; most had walked off the job in the heat of outrage, a heat that soon chilled on the picket line in sub-zero weather. By January 15, there was talk of returning to work; the strikers had no funds, no food, no resources.

"The kids went to bed hungry. We were ready to toss in the towel and give up. . . . Everybody was discouraged. All the fight had been drained out of us," a striker later recalled.

In an attempt to whip up flagging morale, Ettor called a mass demonstration outside the largest mill in Lawrence. On January 15, nearly 15,000 workers stood shivering in front of the locked gates; ill-clad strikers stamped numb feet, huddled in ragged coats and listened to speeches by Ettor, Giovannitti, Gurley Flynn, and Thompson.

Even before the speechmaking was over, and the crowd

had started to disperse, the officer in command of local militiamen stationed on the mill roof decided to break up the demonstration by turning fire hoses on the people below. The shock of that frigid water in the arctic temperature roused the strikers to fighting fury; this humiliation was too much. Goaded by the jeers and taunting laughter of the young soldiers manning the hoses, the strikers bombarded them with chunks of ice. They rushed the gates, scaled the walls, and slashed the hoses that ran up to the rooftop from standpipes on the ground. Before that day ended, thirty-six strikers were in jail; many more, clubbed by police and militiamen, suffered bruises and broken heads. When the demonstration finally ended, the people straggled back to their hovels or to the strike hall, seething with terrible anger. The strike possibly would have collapsed that freezing January day, but the dousing they had received from the fire hoses united the workers as never before.

"Better to starve fighting, than to starve working!" they chanted.

The "water treatment" insured a war to the finish between millowners and workers.

"Big Bill" Haywood

Elizabeth Gurley Flynn

Haywood, Moyer, and Pettibone at the time of their trial.

Caruso, Ettore, and Giovannitti under arrest during their trial.

Judge Fremont Smith and jury hearing testimony during Haywood's trial (Steunenberg Case, 1907).

Parade during Lawrence strike, 1912.
Children in picture are textile workers.

WE NEVER FORGET
A LITTLE CHILD
WE CAME FROM LAWRENCE TO FIND A HOME
SOME DAY WE SHALL REMEMBER EXILE !

(Left top) Hoses turned on Lawrence pickets during bitter, wintry weather, 1912.

(Left bottom) Children of the strikers in Lawrence.

Elizabeth Gurley Flynn exhorting Paterson women strikers in 1913.

Paterson silk strikers forming in New York City to march from Christopher Street Ferry to Madison Square Garden (left) at Madison Avenue and 26th Street for Paterson Strike Pageant.

Surrounded by a straw-hatted audience, Elizabeth Gurley Flynn addresses the I.W.W. in a 1914 Memorial Rally in Union Square, New York City.

Near Bisbee, Arizona, 1914, I.W.W. "bindle stiffs" mount a mass picket line. Automobiles belong to law enforcement officers.

11 THE LAWRENCE STRIKE II

THE REALIZATION that the bosses intended to punish the strikers without mercy came a few days after those arrested at the demonstration were hailed before a magistrate on charges that ranged from disorderly conduct to rioting.

Brushing aside objections of IWW attorneys, the judge heard the cases and sentenced the defendants to jail terms of one year. The entire process took only a few hours. When a newspaper reporter mentioned the severity of the sentences, the judge replied, "The only way we can teach that kind anything is to hand out the stiffest punishment possible. If I could, under the law, I would have salted them away for five years."

On January 17, the governor of Massachusetts ordered state militia and state police into Lawrence, to deal with what he described as "an insurrectionary condition."

Many state militia officers were rich young men attending Harvard. One captain told a newsman, "We find this strike duty rather amusing. A lot of us were bored at school. This offers a change, a real change. Besides, we rather enjoy having a fling at these people and putting them in their proper place!"

Despite troops, state police, city police, and hordes of special deputies, the strikers held firm. Big Bill Haywood came to Lawrence on January 21. A huge throng met him at the railroad station and carried him on their shoulders to the town common, where he delivered a speech calling for solidarity. Pointing to a cordon of militiamen with fixed bayonets, Big Bill roared, "Their weapon is the bayonet! Yours is solidarity! Stand fast, fellow workers, and those bayonets are less dangerous than toothpicks! Solidarity! That's the stuff!"

Unfortunately, the strikers never quite achieved the solidarity for which Big Bill had called. It was limited on a basis of nationalities. The workers banded together according to ethnic groups.

Never before in the United States had there been a strike such as this. It was the first time so many unskilled, unorganized, foreign-born workers had been involved. That the greenhorns dared to strike at all upset the employers enough. But even more disturbing to them, the Wobblies were leading the strikers.

"Frankly, we're scared stiff," a Lawrence millowner told a reporter. "Who knows where this strike will end? It's common knowledge that the IWW wants to overthrow our system. For all we can tell, this is the beginning of the so-called social revolution those damned Wobblies are always hollering about!"

The Lawrence strikers had foes in many quarters—some in the camp of labor. John Golden, head of the AFL United Textile Workers Union, denounced the walkout as "revolutionary" and "anarchistic." He tried unsuccessfully to undermine Haywood and the other IWW leaders and to take over the conduct of the strike himself.

Samuel Gompers, president of the AFL, declared: "This

is not a strike. . . . It is a class-conscious industrial revolution." Gompers blasted the IWW as "irresponsible wreckers, saboteurs and revolutionaries."

The words of Golden and Gompers pleased Wood and the employers. "We would not be so concerned were this an American-run strike. But what's happening here is dangerous," a mill boss said. "If we don't stop the bohunks here, they'll take over the whole country!"

Although strikers of different nationalities still retained Old World fears, prejudices, and suspicions about each other, the walkout remained almost totally effective. Only the skilled workers who belonged to the AFL and a few hundred native Americans scabbed.

Within the ranks of the strikers, the numerically superior Italians, Germans, and French-Canadians occasionally had differences with Poles, Greeks, Russians, Belgians, and the rest. Sometimes ancient grudges, bred in Europe, flared anew on American soil, but on the whole, the strikers manned the picket lines and kept the plants shut.

During the first fortnight of the strike, there were sharp clashes between strikers and police or militia. Heads were bloodied, eyes blackened, bones broken by rifle butts and riot sticks. The police and militia suffered only a few casualties, but the injured among the strikers numbered well over a hundred.

A few days after Big Bill Haywood's arrival, the police uncovered dynamite caches hidden in three scattered places around Lawrence—a tenement house, an empty lot, and in a shoemaker's shop next door to the print shop where Joe Ettor received his mail. The press immediately charged that the dynamite had been put there by "bloodthirsty anarchists." *The New York Times* righteously editorialized: "The strikers displayed a fiendish lack of humanity which ought to place them beyond the comfort of religion until they have repented."

Amid the bold headlines and accusations, Big Bill calmly pointed out that those blaming the IWW for hiding the dynamite were ignoring one peculiar aspect of the incident.

A special edition of the Hearst-owned newspaper, the *Boston American,* was put on sale in Lawrence with details of the "dynamite plot" even before the explosives had been found.

"Obviously," Big Bill said, "the *Boston American* knew all about it. It's a cinch we didn't tell them. I charge that this is an attempt by our enemies to frame us. But for their overly eager hirelings on the *Boston American,* the scheme might have done us much damage."

The Lawrence police were embarrassed by the Boston paper's bungle. Since the Wobblies clearly were not guilty, the police had to find the real culprits. On January 29, Joseph Breen, a local undertaker and member of the Lawrence school board, was arrested for having planted the dynamite. Although finally convicted, Breen was let off with a small fine. Implicated with him were William Wood, Frederick Atteaux, a Boston businessman, and one D. J. Collins. Eventually, they went on trial as Breen's accomplices. The jurors disagreed about Atteaux, acquitted Wood, and found Collins guilty on a few minor counts. However, Wood had some uncomfortable moments during the hearings.

A man named Ernest Pittman, who admitted selling the dynamite to Breen, alleged that Wood was the "brains behind the whole thing." Breen further involved Wood by testifying that the wool magnate had given him money to do the job.

"Did you not render any other service to my client for which you were paid?" Wood's attorney asked Breen.

"Mister, I'm an undertaker! You can bet your bottom dollar that Wood didn't use me professionally!" Breen snapped.

Despite strong evidence against Wood, the jury let him off. The exposure of the crude frame-up awakened sympathy for the strikers across the country. The press, which had been so quick to condemn the IWW as dynamiters, now turned on the millowners. "Two things are perfectly plain," a national magazine stated. "One is that there was an attempt to discredit the strikers by making it appear that they and their sympathizers were harboring dynamite. . . . The other that large sums of money were passed to Breen without an accounting for what purpose that money was used."

January 29, the day of Breen's arrest, brought a crisis to the IWW and the strikers. Joe Ettor had called a rally during the afternoon. It was the biggest strike meeting yet held. People flocked to hear Ettor, their most popular leader.

Arturo Giovannitti was another speaker that day. The young Italian poet had turned his energies to setting up a relief system for the strikers. Under his direction, soup kitchens had been established. Food packages were distributed to families. Funds were raised nationally. Sympathizers sent enough money for the strike committee to dole out a few dollars weekly to each striker. A labor historian noted: "In the Lawrence strike . . . the problem of relief was so efficiently handled that during the entire ten weeks of its duration, there was little wavering . . . in the strikers' ranks."

Ettor's rally was a great success, and when the meeting concluded, he led the strikers on a march through the business district, past the closed mills. A militia company barred the road near one plant and refused to let the marchers go on. For several minutes a serious clash seemed inevitable. However, Ettor averted trouble by waving the strikers into a side street. Arms linked, laughing and singing, the strikers trudged off, without giving the troopers an excuse to attack them.

That evening, tragedy struck. Anna Lo Pizzo, a young striker, was shot dead when special deputies charged a picket line. Although eyewitnesses blamed the killing on a deputy, the police arrested Ettor and Giovannitti, who were more than three miles away at the time. They were charged as accessories to murder because they had advocated mass picketing. Perhaps, in this way, the police sought to deprive the strikers of leadership. A militant striker, Joe Caruso, was seized for the actual crime. Caruso, the police alleged, had fired at the deputies but hit Miss Lo Pizzo by accident.

The tensions in Lawrence were at the breaking point. Mass violence seemed likely to explode any moment. The colonel commanding the militia issued an order: "If necessary, shoot to kill! We are not looking for peace at this time!" He also warned his troops not to salute the Stars and Stripes if borne by "strikers, anarchists, reds, or IWWs." Commented a New York newsman: "Nothing is certain up here in Lawrence except that the Colonel is a full-fledged idiot!"

The militia, made up of businessmen, professionals, college students, and young swashbucklers looking for action, reminded an observer of the vigilantes who had attacked the Wobblies during the free-speech fights out West. The soldiers displayed the same zeal in charging picket lines, rifle butts swinging and bayonets glinting. Cavalry troopers vigorously used sabers, whips, and clubs to scatter crowds of strikers that often included women and children.

Although violence in Lawrence was widespread during the strike, only two fatalities resulted. Besides Miss Lo Pizzo, an eighteen-year-old youth, John Rami, was bayoneted to death by a soldier.

Ettor, Giovannitti, and Caruso remained five months in prison without bail or trial. When the case finally came to court, the proceedings were held in Salem, Massachusetts, the site of the 1692 witchcraft trials. A reporter covering the case wrote:

> It would be impossible to find a more suitable locale. The Massachusetts authorities are repeating the witchcraft trials. The three defendants are brought in to court daily locked

> in portable cages . . . a stunt, I am sure, that is supposed to convince the jurors that these men are desperate characters. . . . Today's unfortunate witches do not ride brooms; they are disguised as Wobblies and locked up like wild animals.

In the period before and during the trial, the IWW carried on large scale agitation for the acquittal of the "Lawrence Three."

Despite the prosecution's high-powered tactics, the state had no solid case against the trio. As one commentator noted: "No jury made up of civilized men could possibly find for the prosecution. . . . The state has based its case on lies, hearsay, hot air and bunkum."

His observations proved correct. The jury brought in a verdict of "Not guilty." Later, one of the jurors said: "We knew that what we were doing wasn't going to sit pretty with the Wool Trust, but the men on the jury figured we had to live with our own consciences. . . . You don't send innocent people to prison."

THAT WINTER OF 1912 AND VICTORY

As THE LAWRENCE strike dragged on through one of the coldest New England winters within living memory, the IWW appealed to the American working class for support. In Lawrence itself, the skilled workers—weavers and loom fixers—walked out in sympathy with the strikers and in defiance of the United Textile Workers Union to which they belonged.

Big Bill Haywood saw Lawrence as a springboard for something much bigger—the One Big Strike toward which the Wobblies were striving. Perhaps Lawrence was the spark that would enflame the American workers and bring on the downfall of the economic and social system.

Although the strikers were not aware that they were in the van of the American "revolution," they did realize that this struggle had deeper implications than wages, hours and working conditions.

A magazine writer summed it up in these words:

> Whatever its future, the IWW has accomplished one tre-

> mendous big thing . . . that is the individual awakening of "illiterates" and "scum". . . to the realization of their dignity and rights in this, or any other society. . . . They have learned . . . consciousness of self.

This was stated far more succinctly on placards carried by young women strikers during a Lawrence demonstration. Scrawled on the picket signs was the phrase: WE WANT BREAD AND ROSES TOO!

To help them win both bread and roses, the IWW called upon workingmen everywhere to help the "embattled slaves of Lawrence." Speaking at a strike meeting Haywood stated: "If we prevail on other workers who handle your goods to go on strike, we will tie up the railroads, put the city in darkness and starve the soldiers out."

No general strike came over Lawrence. American workers were not yet ready for action of that radical nature, although the Wobblies constantly called upon "fellow workers . . . everywhere" to lend a hand. They urged a nation-wide boycott of Lawrence. An appeal in the *Industrial Worker* headed "Boycott Lawrence!" said: "Railroad men: lose their freight cars for them! Telegraphers: lose their messages for them! Expressmen: lose their packages for them! Against the bludgeon of Industrial Despotism, bring the silent might of Industrial Democracy!"

If American workers did not heed the general-strike plea and failed to boycott Lawrence, they stood shoulder-to-shoulder with the strikers on a side issue stemming from the walkout.

As the winter of 1912 worsened, the striking workers and their families suffered agonizing deprivations. The two or three dollars per week from the strike relief fund could not buy clothing or coal. Despite the IWW soup kitchens and the food parcels handed out by the Strike Relief, hunger stalked the working-class sections of Lawrence. Children, especially, were feeling the effects of cold and malnutrition.

The strike committee hit upon a desperate measure. After much painful deliberation it was decided to send strikers' children to sympathizers in other cities, to be cared for until the trouble was over. This tactic had been used successfully in Europe by French, Belgian, and Italian strikers.

Arrangements were made with families in New York City to accept 150 Lawrence children. On February 10, the group left Lawrence by train for Grand Central Station in New York. At the depot, they were met by more than 5,000 members of the Italian Socialist Federation and the American Socialist Party. The wan, pale children were whisked away to homes in Manhattan and Brooklyn, where well-meaning "foster parents" heaped them with more food, clothing, candy, and toys than the youngsters ever had seen in their lives.

Among those accompanying the children was Margaret Sanger, a nurse, who went on to become famous for her work in the field of birth control. Mrs. Sanger later described the condition of her charges: "Out of the 150 children, only four had underwear. . . . Their outerwear was almost in rags . . . their coats were torn to shreds . . . and it was the bitterest weather we had all winter."

With the arrival of the "Lawrence refugees," outsiders had their first actual view of conditions in Lawrence. When the children trooped off the train and shuffled listlessly into the station, a cry went up from the spectators, "A cry of horror, outrage and sorrow," said one reporter. Many wept at the sight of those "half-starved waifs." Even the conservative newspapers that had been almost solidly against the IWW and the strike, now changed their tunes and blasted the wool magnates.

Famous journalists, among them Ray Stannard Baker, Mary Heaton Vorse, and William Allen White, went to Lawrence and wrote scathing criticisms of what they found in that unhappy city. William Allen White wrote: "In my entire life, I have never seen more heart-rending sights than in Lawrence. . . . Oh, the children! The poor, suffering, innocent children!"

Nothing the IWW could have done proved more valuable to the strikers than the evacuation of the children. But the Lawrence police and the Massachusetts militia provided an even greater bonus to the Wobblies and the strikers with a display of wanton callousness seldom matched by the authorities of any American city.

Two weeks after the first migration of the children, a second group of 150 was being sent to Philadelphia. As the youngsters and their mothers were waiting at the Lawrence railroad station, a force of fifty policemen and two militia companies suddenly charged down on them with clubs and rifle butts. Mothers and children alike were knocked insensible. An onlooker recalled that "the snow was stained red with blood. . . . I could not believe this was happening in America. It was a scene worthy of Czarist Russia at its tyrannical worst."

The brutal attack on the women and children stirred a hurricane of protest. Even Senator William Borah, who had prosecuted Big Bill Haywood at Boise in 1907, voiced his indignation at this "violation of constitutional privilege." The AFL's Samuel Gompers, an avowed enemy of the Wobblies, denounced the attack as "a crime" and asked, "Have the officials of Lawrence lost their minds to permit such an atrocity?"

The men who controlled the Wool Trust were vicious, but not stupid. William Wood and his cohorts recognized that mass opinion was turning against them. Early in March, it became a tidal wave when Congress investigated the Lawrence strike. The image of the American Woolen Company was badly tarnished as young workers testified that their employer held back a week's pay, that the company forced them to do unpaid cleanup work on Saturdays, and that, in order to get decent drinking water, they had to pay as much as ten cents a week bribe to their foremen.

National ire was at fever pitch. Mrs. William Howard Taft, the First Lady, never before noted for social awareness, was so moved by the plight of the Lawrence workers that she attended every meeting of the House committee conducting the investigation.

The Cleveland *News*, an influential paper, railed editorially against an industry "enjoying tariffs of 40 percent to 150 percent as protection against the pauper labor of Europe, which pays only $6.00 to $8.00 per week for the labor of American workers."

Faced by this mounting resentment, the American Woolen Company capitulated on March 12, 1912, and granted all the strikers' demands. By the end of March, the rest of the wool companies surrendered. The wages and working conditions of textile workers throughout New England were raised.

And, on March 30, with bands playing and banners flying, the evacuated children returned home. Even as they were arriving, militia units crept silently out of town; special deputies turned in their badges, guns, and clubs; and, according to eyewitnesses, "there wasn't a single cop in sight at the railroad station when the kids alighted."

The IWW had scored a rousing victory. After the strike, the Lawrence local grew to 14,000 members. Only a few months earlier it had numbered only two hundred. However, the employers eventually had the final word. A fifty-percent speedup of the mill machines practically wiped out the wage increases gained in the strike settlement. The workers were too exhausted by the long struggle to protest or take any positive action. By 1914, the local was down to only four hundred members.

As in the past, the Wobblies proved to be good fighters but poor builders. They could win immediate demands, but lacked the patience needed for developing a strong organization after the battle was over. As one Wobbly explained, "We no longer cared about victories already won. There always was another struggle to be fought elsewhere."

Although the IWW failed to hold the gains the strikers had won, their Lawrence triumph heartened workers in other eastern cities and set the stage for an even greater strike drama in the Paterson, New Jersey, silk mills.

Even more important, the Lawrence strike revealed to a shocked American public the awful conditions under which many thousands of immigrants were forced to earn their bread. Lawrence prickled the conscience of the United States and awakened many Americans to the dismal truth that their country was no paradise, especially for minority groups.

THE PATERSON STRIKE I

IN 1913, PATERSON, NEW JERSEY, was a grimy industrial city sprawling gracelessly on the banks of the Passaic River. It had a population of 123,000 persons, including numerous Italian, German, and Slavic immigrants, most of whom worked in Paterson's silk industry.

The city, known as the Lyons of America because of its nearly three hundred silk mills, had long been restive as working conditions worsened in the mills. Located only fifteen miles from New York City, Paterson had an undeserved reputation as a hotbed of anarchism because a small group of Italian anarchists lived and worked there. Actually, Paterson was no more radical than any other American city.

Of the 73,000 working people in Paterson, about 25,000 were employed in the silk mills. Their average workday was ten hours and the salary of an average millhand ran from $9.00 to $12.00 weekly. However, some women earned less than $8.00, and girls under sixteen received only $3.00.

In the winter, workers had to wear overcoats on the job because the ramshackle frame buildings were unheated.

During the summer months, men and women were felled by heat. The air in the workrooms was stifling. Artificial humidifiers were used to produce the required dampness needed for silk weaving. Steam and acid fumes so choked dye houses that the dyers could barely make out those working next to them. The incidence of tuberculosis and other respiratory diseases ran extremely high among Paterson silk workers.

The millowners had decided, early in 1911, to reduce production costs by increasing from two to four the number of looms an operator must handle. Automatic high-speed looms that were simple to run had been introduced at the turn of the century. With such machinery readily available, the employers envisioned greater output and higher profits at lower expense.

The workers objected to the new methods. Running two machines was difficult enough; to operate four would be an almost unbearable speedup. This was not the only grievance of Paterson millhands. They protested a number of abuses such as the "kickback" racket of the foremen who demanded a weekly payment from each worker under the threat of being fired. "We were paying blackmail. If you didn't come across with a couple of cents each week, the foremen would can you on the spot and tell the front office you'd been loafing on the job," a Paterson millhand recalled.

The workers also sought an end to the inequity of several wage scales in the same shop for the same job. They wanted the eight-hour day as well. Working hours had not been adjusted since 1904.

When the first mill adopted the four-loom system in 1911, some workers angrily stalked out. A few belonged to the United Textile Workers Union, but most were unorganized. The UTW president, John Golden, rushed to Paterson and persuaded the men to return, promising that the dispute would be arbitrated.

The strikers went back but the four-loom system remained. Many silk workers accused Golden of having "sold out" to the employers. However, he called the four-loom system "a technological advance for the silk industry" and warned that "disciplinary action of a serious nature" would be taken against any UTW member who "agitated, demonstrated or took part in any work stoppage, strike or act of sabotage."

Golden's high-handed treatment of the workers brought on a wholesale withdrawal from the UTW and opened the way for the Wobblies when big trouble hit Paterson on January 27, 1913, over the four-loom issue.

That day a committee called on the management of the Doherty Silk Mill to talk over elimination or modification of the four-loom system. The delegates were refused an audience with the management and fired forthright. This so incensed the company's eight hundred employees that they called a strike against Doherty. Within a month, the walkout had become industry-wide. By February 25, more than 25,000 workers were out, effectively shutting down all three hundred of Paterson's mills.

The strike committee called in the IWW to lead their struggle; the Wobblies still basked in the afterglow of the Lawrence victory. Three IWW stalwarts—Elizabeth Gurley Flynn; Carlo Tresca, a militant organizer; and Pat Quinlan, coal miner, longshoreman, sailor, and fiery orator—came to Paterson on February 25 to address a strike rally. Miss Flynn, Tresca, and Quinlan did not disappoint the audience. Each delivered a ringing speech, each promised the strikers the fullest support of the IWW and the working class.

Just after the meeting adjourned, Miss Flynn, Tresca, and Quinlan were arrested on open charges. Paterson's mayor, Andrew McBride, stated that the arrests were made in accordance with "the ancient right of cities to rid themselves of undesirables." However, this was not enough to warrant jailing the three Wobblies. They were released with a warning to "get out of Paterson or take the consequences." The three unanimously chose the latter course.

A Paterson police official told a reporter, "We've no objection to our own people conducting a strike, but we'll not put up with outside agitators. . . . The IWW better take heed for their own good. We want no crackpot anarchists here."

But the Wobblies did not quit Paterson. Instead they dug in more deeply. Big Bill Haywood came to town and was fervidly greeted by the strikers. Fresh from a strike of rubber workers in Akron, Ohio, Big Bill gave a rousing talk to the Paterson strikers. "Remember our slogan: 'An Injury to One Is an Injury to All.' We must stand united for victory or we shall fail miserably!" Big Bill's dynamic presence and the bright aura of the Lawrence strike made him a legendary figure to the silk workers. In their eyes, Big Bill and the IWW could do no wrong.

Haywood proudly boasted to a magazine writer, "There's a red card in the home of every silk striker." This was almost true. Thousands of the strikers joined the IWW. But, according to the writer, "So hard is the grip of poverty on the workers that many have remained outside the organization that is conducting their fight simply to save the dues of thirty cents a month."

If the Paterson strikers embraced several different nationalities, they also had loyalties to groups other than the IWW. Within their ranks were socialists, followers of De Leon, anarchists, and some AFL unionists.

Each branch of the silk industry employed workers of a particular national origin. For example, ribbon weavers invariably were American citizens, naturalized or native born. Silk weavers and dyers tended to be non-English-speaking Italians, Germans, or Slavs. The unskilled jobs were handled by the wives and children of workers from every part of Europe and the Middle East.

If ever a melting pot existed it was in Paterson; seldom had striking workers been as divided by nationality, religion, and politics than were those in Paterson. By all precedents the strike should have ended swiftly in a welter of internal bickering and dissension. That it did not, that the strike held firm from February, 1913, until July, was due to the Wobblies who welded the diverse groups into a solid, united front.

Paterson strikers faced the usual ruthless repression from police, militia, and private company guards. The latter were the most vicious; they roved the streets in groups and used blackjacks and revolver butts on any strikers that crossed their path. The guards shot and killed two workers—one in a picket line clash; the other, Valentino Modestino, was slain while sitting with his child on the steps of a house across the street from a strikebound silk mill. Although three company guards were arrested for these shootings, none ever was tried.

More than 15,000 strikers turned out for the funerals of the murder victims. They marched through the heart of Paterson in a procession that stretched more than a mile. The caskets were heaped high with red carnations silently dropped on them by the mourners. Big Bill, Miss Flynn, and Carlo Tresca delivered moving eulogies at the graveside.

Despite the violence (seven strikers killed during the course of the strike), despite mass arrests (more than 100 strikers hauled in daily), despite harsh jail sentences (ten to thirty days in the overcrowded, unsanitary Passaic County prison), despite the imprisonment of strike leaders (Pat Quinlan served in jail from 1913 to 1915 on charges of "inciting to riot"), the silk workers of Paterson refused to yield.

At a huge rally, thousands of them pledged to hold out until all their demands were met. What they were asking seemed modest enough: an eight-hour day, a minimum wage of $16.00 for skilled and $12.00 for unskilled workers, the abolition of the four-loom system, no retaliation against union militants, and amnesty for all arrested strikers.

"We're simply trying to bring Paterson out of the Stone Ages," a strike leader stated.

According to the workers, the millowners seemed to lack the same desire and fought with all their resources to break the strike. The best allies they had were the two Paterson daily newspapers as well as most of New York City's press. The local afternoon paper ran front-page editorials urging the formation of vigilante committees to "get rid of the Red agitators plaguing our city . . . and to scatter the picket lines that are strangling our economy."

"Are there not in Paterson 1,000 real Americans who will march against the radicals destroying the serenity of our beloved city? Must we be subjected to the tyranny of foreign philosophies? Must we knuckle under to the human refuse that swarmed down upon our shores from every pesthole in Europe? We think not! Americans, awake!" screamed a Paterson *Press* editorial.

Vigilante bands were formed. Armed with police power, these "real" Americans—many of whom were petty criminals, local toughs, and hoodlums—launched a terror campaign against the strikers. Men were beaten, hosed down with streams of water, and left to freeze in the wintry weather that persisted far into spring that year. Strikers' homes were burned; union halls wrecked; children mistreated. And still the strike went on.

THE PATERSON STRIKE II

THE YEAR 1913 had no spring on the East Coast; in mid-April, winter suddenly gave way to blazing summer. Within twenty-four hours, the thermometer soared from near freezing into the high eighties. Day after day the sun beat down. A record heat wave gripped the entire area.

The change in climate brought no comfort to the strikers. Perishable food collected in strike headquarters spoiled during those sweltering days because there was no refrigeration. Difficulties mounted. For some reason a near-epidemic of upper respiratory infection swept through the strikers' ranks. The few volunteer doctors who had donated their services were unable to cope with the number of cases. As the unseasonable weather continued, parents grew concerned that their undernourished children might be stricken by polio.

Then, to add to the strikers' woes, Paterson officials forbade public meetings within city limits. This necessitated a march to the neighboring town of Haledon, which had a Socialist mayor who allowed strike rallies to be held there.

Every Sunday, thousands of Paterson workers trudged the few miles to Haledon, where they assembled on a residential street.

A strike sympathizer who owned a two-story house allowed speakers to use a second-floor porch that overlooked the street and made a fine platform for speechmakers.

The Sunday rallies featured pep talks by such notables as Miss Gurley Flynn, Tresca, Big Bill, and others, a concert by a makeshift band, group singing of Wobbly songs, and various kinds of entertainment. The Haledon meetings always attracted visitors from New York City—students, writers, artists, actors, liberals, and radicals—with money, food, and clothing collected from strike supporters in the city.

(One emotional high spot of the strike was the large-scale evacuation of children to New York and Brooklyn. As with the Lawrence youngsters, the sight of the forlorn, wretched refugees wrenched hearts and aroused sympathy for the strikers.)

The apogee of the Paterson strike was a pageant staged in Madison Square Garden, then located on 26th Street and Madison Avenue, in New York City. The spectacle made the strike one of the most notable labor disputes of the twentieth century. The initiator of the Paterson pageant was a handsome, burly, twenty-four-year-old journalist named John (Jack) Reed, Harvard, class of 1910.

Young Reed, who lived in Greenwich Village and worked for *American* Magazine, belonged to a group of arty "bohemians" known as "New Intellectuals," radicals both in viewpoint and behavior. Reed heard firsthand about the Paterson strike from Bill Haywood, whom he met at a Greenwich Village party. So impressed was Reed that he decided to go out to Paterson and take a look for himself. On a rainy April day, he took an early-morning train to the strike city and there got "an eyeful."

While he was talking to some strikers on a stoop, a policeman ordered Reed to move on.

"I'm doing nothing wrong," he said. "I've a right to stand here!"

"I said *move* and I mean *move!*" the officer snarled. "If you don't hop it, I'll run you in!"

"Go ahead! Arrest me!" Reed challenged.

The policeman complied. Reed was collared, taken to court, and sentenced to a twenty-day jail term. Tossed into a four-by-seven-foot cell, the Harvard man found himself sharing the cramped quarters with eight strikers, some of whom had gone without food or water for an entire day.

The New York evening newspapers had a field day with the story of the Harvard alumnus jailed with fifty pickets who had been run in at the same time. Among that batch of prisoners were Big Bill Haywood and Carlo Tresca. The Wobbly leaders gave Reed quick courses in revolutionary unionism during brief walks around the prison yard.

After four days, Reed had had enough of prison life and permitted a Harvard classmate to bail him out. By then, he was daily front-page copy. Every newspaper ran stories about the college boy and the greenhorn strikers. The Paterson chief of police complained, "They're making more fuss over that Harvard snob than the hundreds of pickets I've locked up."

Reed, burning to do "something big" for the Paterson strikers, returned to New York. "Jack was a man possessed," a friend remembered. "He could talk only of the strike, the strikers, their courage and sacrifice."

He did not limit himself to talking. Always persuasive, Reed induced a number of his friends to attend a Sunday meeting at Haledon. They, too, were impressed by the strikers and their cause. (Among Reed's intimates were several young men who would gain fame in their chosen fields: Walter Lippmann, the columnist; Edmund Hunt, writer and editor; Hutchins Hapgood, drama critic and founder of the Provincetown Playhouse; Robert Edmond Jones, stage designer; and John Sloan, artist. In 1913, they were young and unknown.)

With this group plus other artists, writers, actors, musicians, designers, and playwrights who frequented the elegant lower Fifth Avenue home of Mabel Dodge, a wealthy divorcee, Reed conceived the idea of a gigantic pageant to dramatize the strike, give the strikers valuable publicity, and raise funds for them.

Mrs. Dodge, a dabbler in modern art, radical causes, and bohemianism, also had a passionate interest in Jack Reed. She showed her devotion to him by putting her wealth and influence at his disposal. Through the generosity of Mrs. Dodge, Reed and his colleagues gathered enough cash to rent Madison Square Garden for one evening and to finance a single performance of the pageant.

No amount of money could have hired the talented people who volunteered their services and created the Paterson Pageant. The artist John Sloan painted the scenery, featuring a tremendous canvas backdrop upon which was portrayed a huge silk mill flanked by two smaller ones. Robert Edmond Jones designed the setting.

If everyone connected with the production was busy, Jack Reed was a human dynamo. He wrote the pageant, a moving spectacle divided into six episodes to be enacted by strikers and their leaders. Big Bill Haywood, Carlo Tresca, and Miss Gurley Flynn would give the actual speeches they had made during the strike.

The performance was scheduled for Saturday evening, June 7, which meant a lot had to be accomplished in about three weeks' time. Reed spent that period training one thousand strikers to reenact strike scenes. He also conducted them in Wobbly songs and an original one he had composed to the tune of "Harvard, Old Harvard."

The three weeks sped by. Reed worked himself into a state of near exhaustion, but somehow kept going. At last the big day arrived. During the afternoon of June 7, several thousand strikers boarded a special fourteen-car train in Paterson, got off at Hoboken, and proceeded to New York City via the Christopher Street Ferry.

From the ferryhouse, they marched up Fifth Avenue with red flags in the van, IWW banners raised high, and several Wobbly bands blaring the "Internationale," "The Marseillaise," "Hold the Fort," "Solidarity Forever!," and "Hallelujah I'm a Bum." New York's mayor, William J. Gaynor, a shrewd politician, extended the strikers every courtesy and provided a police escort for the parade to Madison Square Garden.

After a run-through during the late afternoon, the pageant was ready. Scheduled to start at 7:00 P.M., it had to be delayed an hour until the 15,000 spectators cleared the aisles and found their seats.

Although the Garden was filled to capacity, the committee was distressed. While seats for $.50 and $2.25 sold out, those priced at $1.50 and $2.00 had barely moved. As a last resort, to ensure a full house, these places were sold for what they could bring and many hundreds of Wobblies gained free admittance by showing their red cards.

Seated in a box near the stage was Julius Harburger, the sheriff of New York County. "Just let anybody say one word of disrespect to the flag and I'll stop the show so quickly it'll take their breath away," he warned. The sheriff fancied himself a guardian of Americanism and frequently had spoken out against "sedition, treasonable utterances, and un-American doctrines."

The crowds streaming into the Garden gawked at a huge electric sign that formed the letters IWW ten feet high atop the tower of the block-long arena. The bright red electric lights stood out vividly against the night sky and could be seen for miles around.

Jack Reed had stated the purpose of the show in the program: "The pageant represents a battle between the working class and the capitalist class conducted by the Industrial Workers of the World. . . . It is a conflict between two social forces."

Those present in the Garden that night underwent a searing emotional experience. According to one newspaper:

> Fifteen thousand spectators applauded with shouts and tears the Great Paterson Strike Pageant at Madison Square Garden. . . . The scenes unrolled with a poignant realism that no man who saw them will ever forget.

Reed and his friends had come through splendidly. The pageant recaptured the essence of the strike, depicting the opening walkout at the Doherty Mill, the shrieking plant whistles, the din of machinery, the clashes with the police, the funeral of Valentino Modestino, and the graveside speeches by Haywood, Tresca, and Gurley Flynn.

Everyone agreed that the reenactment of Modestino's funeral was the dramatic highlight of the evening. Pallbearers carrying a coffin moved down the aisle through the audience. Behind them came more than a thousand strikers singing a funeral march composed for the occasion.

The dead man's widow was sitting in a box close to the stage. When she saw the coffin, Mrs. Modestino shrieked hysterically, adding an unrehearsed note of realism to the proceedings. The mourners heaped the casket with red carnations as they had done at the actual rites. Big Bill, Carlo Tresca, and Miss Gurley Flynn repeated the touching eulogies they had delivered at the grave.

Many in the audience wept during the scene. Mrs. Dodge noted that "for a few electric moments there was a terrible unity between all those people. They were one: the workers who had come to show their comrades what was happening across the river and the workers who had come to see it. I have never felt such . . . a vibration in any gathering before or since."

At the performance's end, the audience rose spontaneously to sing the "Internationale." Reed's friend, Hutchins Hapgood, the drama critic for the New York *Globe,* wrote ecstatically: "Such self-expression . . . among the masses may become a rich reality, spreading a human glow over the whole of humanity . . . from which we shall all be gainers, in life, in justice, in art, in love."

These high-flown sentiments and hopes were not realized. The truth was that, despite its propagandistic and artistic merits, the pageant was a failure. Instead of making money for the strikers, it had a deficit. Receipts came to $7,645.45; expenses, $9,641.95; a loss of $1,996.50. A one-night performance at Madison Square Garden had been too expensive. The anticipated collection fell far below expectations because the audience, mostly workers, could not afford to contribute much money. (Unfounded accusations of "crooked" accounting caused hard feelings and gave the hostile press the chance to insinuate that the committee, "far from being altruistic, lined their pockets.")

Even worse than such talk were the petty jealousies the pageant had stirred among the strikers. Those who had stayed behind to man the picket lines were bitter against those who had taken part in the show. What had been conceived as a noble project ended with squabbling and dissension.

Jack Reed missed all the unpleasantness. A few days after the performance he sailed for Venice with Mrs. Dodge and Robert Edmond Jones. Big Bill Haywood, suffering from an attack of stomach ulcers, also left for Europe.

The strike limped along until July. The effort of putting on the pageant seemed to have taken all the starch out of the strikers. Outside sympathizers felt that by attending the show they had fulfilled all obligations to the silk workers. Donations of money and food dwindled away. Sensing that the workers were weakening, the employers applied even greater pressure. They not only increased arrests of pickets, but also used more subtle forms of persuasion.

The millowners offered to deal with the strikers on a shop-by-shop basis of settlement, rather than an industry-wide one as the IWW had insisted. Tired, hungry, discouraged, some strikers snatched at the offer; their magnificent solidarity crumbled and collapsed. United for nearly five months, they were fragmented into shop units. Worn out by the long struggle, they limped back to work under virtually the same miserable conditions that had been in effect before the strike.

Speedups continued, union men were fired, wages remained low, and the Wobblies, riding high in Paterson, lost favor with the workers. There were other strikes in Paterson after 1913, but the IWW led none of them.

The great Paterson strike concluded in defeat for the mill-hands, but the determination and fortitude they displayed served for years as an inspiration to the American labor movement. The IWW came away without victory, but not without honor. Paterson ranked with Lawrence and other great American labor upheavals such as Homestead, the Pullman Strike, and the Haymarket Massacre. As always, the Wobblies had been giants in combat and less than pygmies in the task of forging a well-based, smoothly running organization.

Individualists from top to bottom, they mistrusted authority even within their own ranks. As a labor historian noted, "The IWW always carried democracy one step too far. . . .

After the Everett Massacre, a Wobbly was asked, 'Who is your leader?' The reply came, '*We're all leaders!*' If the IWW had one fatal flaw—that was it."

At Lawrence and at Paterson, this defect proved crippling. The concept of collective leadership simply did not work among immigrant laborers who needed and had been accustomed to strong guidance. The greenhorns of the East differed from the footloose bindle stiffs of the West. The former had grown up in the clime of tyranny and did not know how to handle freedom. The latter had been free and independent all their lives and resented any sort of restraint.

This contradiction eventually destroyed the IWW; by seeking to please every man, it succeeded in pleasing none. The noble motives of the Wobblies eroded after Paterson and there followed a period of internal bickering that spread like a cancerous growth, wasting and rotting what once had been a potentially healthy body.

THE "COOLIES" OF AMERICA

DURING THE PATERSON strike, the IWW was involved in other sectors of the labor front and made inroads among rubber workers, auto workers, and Southern lumber workers in Louisiana and Mississippi, where blacks and whites belonged to the same locals. This was one of the first instances of integration in any union.

The Wobbly attempts to unionize in auto and rubber met only partial success. It would not be until the 1930's that these industries became unionized. Back in 1913, the IWW lacked both funds and manpower to carry on sustained organizational drives in those fields.

However, the Wobblies had blazed the trail for another generation of unionists. No matter how involved the IWW was in mass struggles, it never abandoned the dream of One Big Union or failed to respond when workers called for help.

In August, 1913, such an appeal was heard in California; a plea from the downtrodden men and women who picked hops during the harvest season. These were among the lowest-paid and most mistreated workers in the country. A newspaperman dubbed the hop pickers "the coolies of America."

A dramatic confrontation between hop pickers and hop growers took place at Wheatland, California, located between Marysville and Sacramento. E. B. Durst, a hop grower, reputed to be the largest single employer of migratory workers in the state, advertised in the newspapers for a force of 2,700 pickers.

By July 30, 1913, nearly three thousand men, women, and children flocked to the Durst ranch, camping on a sun-baked hillside. They had come in response to the ad. Many had walked miles to get there, only to find that Durst had called for nearly twice as many workers as he needed so that he could hire those willing to work for the lowest pay.

The best Durst offered was an average of $1.28 per day. From this paltry sum was deducted a daily fee of $.75 for the rental of a tent to shelter the worker and his family. Those who did not choose to pay that much could rent a pile of straw to sleep on at $.75 per week. Most slept on bare ground.

Sanitary conditions at Durst's camp were ghastly. Only nine outdoor toilets served the three thousand people gathered there. Cooking facilities were of the crudest; irrigation ditches soon were choked with garbage, and a foul, nauseating stench hung over the campsite. Dysentery reached near-epidemic proportions.

Working conditions were as primitive as those under which the hop pickers lived. The work day started at 4:00 A.M. and continued uninterrupted for ten hours. Men, women, and children stumbled out into the fields in predawn darkness and toiled all day in heat that often exceeded 105 degrees.

There was no drinking water in the field and a lemonade wagon—owned by Durst's cousin—supplied the thirsty pickers with stale lemon water at $.05 a glass. Durst would not permit any of the shopkeepers in the surrounding area to deliver food into the camp. The migrants were forced to buy their groceries at a Durst-run store on the premises at prices far steeper than those outside.

Only about a hundred of the three thousand hop pickers ever had had any contact with the IWW. Of this group, about thirty were active Wobblies. Within three days after arriving in camp, these men assumed leadership over the rest. A mass meeting on Saturday, August 2, elected a committee to present Durst with a list of demands. The pickers wanted free drinking water brought out to them twice a day, the right to buy food off the Durst premises, sufficient toilets with separate facilities for men and women, showers, garbage dumps, free tents, a raise in pay, and overtime after eight hours.

Two of the committee members, Dick (Blackie) Ford and Herman Suhr, were veterans of the Fresno and San Diego free-speech fights. They served as spokesmen for the delegation that went to Durst. Instead of negotiating, Durst flew into a rage, slapped Ford in the face, and ordered the committee men off his property in twenty-four hours. "Or else, you damned Wobbly troublemakers, you'll leave here in a pine box," Durst shouted.

The next day, Sunday, August 3, the Wobblies called a mass meeting at a Wheatland public dance hall they had rented for the purpose. Speaking to more than two thousand workers, Blackie Ford took a sick baby from the mother's arms and held up the mewling infant for all to see. "It's not for ourselves we must take action, but for the kids!" he cried.

Just then, two carloads of sheriff's deputies roared up to

arrest Ford. One of the deputies, "obviously drunk," according to an eyewitness, fired a shot over the heads of the crowd. A wild melee suddenly broke out.

Screaming women and children fled wildly in all directions. Shouting and cursing men swarmed over the deputies. Fists flew, chairs went sailing through the air, shots crackled. The uproar lasted only a few minutes. When it ended, the Marysville district attorney, a deputy sheriff, and two workers were dead. Dozens of others had been injured or wounded.

The frightened hop pickers cleared out of the Durst place. The roads were clogged with migrants trying to get away, but citizen vigilantes attacked the fleeing bindle stiffs. When Governor Hiram W. Johnson heard of the Wheatland incident, he rushed five companies of militia there "to overawe any labor demonstration and protect private property."

Detectives hired by the Hop Growers Association rounded up hundreds of suspected Wobblies throughout California and neighboring states. The prisoners were held incommunicado, beaten, and tortured. So savage was the treatment accorded them that one Wobbly went insane and another committed suicide in prison.

The severest punishment was dealt to Blackie Ford and Herman Suhr. Charged with leading the demonstration that brought on the killings, they were convicted of second-degree murder in a trial held eight months later. Sentenced to life imprisonment, they were finally paroled in 1923 after serving ten years of that term.

The so-called Wheatland Hop Riot was a significant event in the long history of California's labor troubles. The first such outbreak among migratory workers, it focused a national spotlight on the intolerable conditions among agricultural workers in California and inspired the IWW to undertake what seemed an impossible mission—the organization of agricultural migratory workers.

"Anybody with sense would have quit that game before he started," an IWW leader noted. "But we Wobblies were long on sympathy and short on logic. We wanted to help the poor bindle stiffs who worked the harvest fields and so we plunged right in and got on with the task."

The IWW began with the migratories in California. Less than a year after the Wheatland Hop Riot, forty new IWW locals had sprung up in the Golden Bear State. The Wobblies advised men to organize on the job and to "sabotage" the work if their demands were not met. IWW stickers were pasted on walls and buildings, on cars and windows; from one end of California to the other, no one could doubt the presence of the Wobblies.

Although there was some violence, some crop burnings and sabotage, a federal government investigation could find little to connect the IWW with the arson that plagued California farmers and others who hired migratory workers.

One investigator noted:

> The IWW will not be suppressed until first are throttled those conditions on which it feeds. Employers like Durst who shriek the loudest against the IWW are the very ones whose absolute disregard of the rights of others, and whose oppressions and inhumanities are more potent crusaders to swell the ranks of the IWW than its most ardent propagandists.

The September, 1914, convention of the IWW formally urged that "concerted and effective action should be taken in the harvest fields." This was enthusiastically approved. A new era was dawning for the army of bindle stiffs whose ranks were daily growing as many thousands of industrial workers, thrown out of a job by the 1914 depression, were riding freights in search of work in the harvest fields.

According to one historian: "American radicalism in the form of the IWW spread rapidly among these men."

The Wobblies created a new group, the Agricultural Workers Organization (AWO), with headquarters in Kansas City and later in Minneapolis. From these headquarters eager young organizers went forth, men hardened in free-speech fights and on a hundred picket lines.

Under the leadership of a genial, blond six-footer named Walter Nef, a German-Swiss who cared nothing for politics and everything for workers—especially those on the bottom of the economic heap, the harvest bindle stiffs—the AWO flourished. Its influence was felt from Kansas to South Dakota, which Nef called "the world's longest picket line."

The Wobbly organizers of the AWO did not agitate on street corners or hold mass meetings. Known as "job" delegates, they signed up men in the field while working alongside them. Each organizer was a "mobile office" carrying with him membership cards, dues books, and IWW literature.

The response to this drive was sensational. The AWO job delegates had little difficulty persuading harvest stiffs to join for better conditions. The situation in the harvest fields was abominable. Men, women, and children worked ten hours a day or longer in temperatures that often soared above one hundred degrees. Their housing was squalid. Bunks crawled with lice and vermin. Washing and toilet facilities were inadequate. The farmers served their fieldhands the cheapest food, dished out in a manner "more suitable to hogs than to human beings," an AWO delegate reported.

Harvest hands were further exploited by employment sharks who charged them $1.00 to $5.00 for jobs that often proved to be nonexistent.

The life of a harvest stiff was uncertain at best. Even at the height of harvest season he rarely earned more than $2.50 per day. As harvests of various crops were ready at the same time, the demand for fieldworkers rose. The stiffs had to hurry from place to place, riding freight cars for transportation. Although work at harvest time was plentiful, there were always four or five people for every available job.

When the wheat crops were gathered, the hands left for the Corn Belt in Iowa and Nebraska and then moved north to the Minnesota potato fields. After the harvest season ended, the bindle stiffs went job-hunting in lumber camps or oil fields, always insecure, always rootless, always wandering.

Without organization they were easy prey for the employers. But with the AWO, they had strength. The AWO demanded higher pay, shorter hours, and better living conditions for harvest stiffs. These usually were won by sudden, sporadic strikes that had to be quickly settled or else a farmer could not have his crop picked, a financial disaster for him. Better to come to terms with the AWO than to let the harvest rot on the ground.

Thanks to the efforts of AWO organizers, the Wheat Belt, the Corn Belt, and the wide agricultural regions of the United States became Wobbly territory. From 1914 to 1917, the AWO grew to a peak of 70,000 members. Red-card-carrying Wobblies ruled the freight trains on which the migratories rode. Often, a red card was recognized as a train ticket by sympathetic railroad men, so that many Wobblies traveled in comfort from harvest to harvest.

It was a colorful time for the IWW; a time when harvest stiffs sang Wobbly songs while working in the field. For once, they felt strong and united, able to cope with any situation, even the violence of the numerous vigilante groups. For once, the harvest stiffs fought back, trading punch for punch, blow for blow, and shot for shot.

When the United States entered World War I in April, 1917, near-hysteria over the IWW "menace" swept farming, mining, and lumbering regions where the Wobblies had grown strong. The federal government banned strikes in "industries vital to the national defense"—specifically naming lumbering, mining, and agriculture.

This edict from Washington gave local authorities license to crack down on the Wobblies. Arrests, beatings, and mass deportations of "radicals" became commonplace. The anti-IWW campaign reached such a frenzy that a liberal newsman wrote: "I believe that the Liberty Bell isn't merely cracked; it has been shattered by those who crush the liberty of men whose opinions differ from theirs."

The AWO, which had brought some dignity and hope to the wretched harvest workers, was permanently crippled in the early fall of 1917, when the government went after the IWW. More than one hundred leading Wobblies were arrested at that time on charges of violating the Espionage Act. The IWW never quite recovered from this setback and the suppression of the postwar years practically finished off the Wobblies by 1924, although a shadow organization has survived to the present day.

When modern farm machinery took over the tasks of harvesting, the need for migratory agricultural workers was greatly curtailed. Nonetheless, there are today thousands of migratory agricultural workers engaged in stoop labor, picking crops that are unsuitable for machine harvest. But the memory of the singing Wobblies, the hard, bold men who faced violence and death to better the lot of fellow workers, never faded completely. It lived on in legend.

Nor can the years erase the fact that from 1905 to 1924,

of the one million red cards issued by the IWW, 100,000 were held by black men. No other union movement before or since has given to black Americans the equality and respect shown them by the Wobblies.

16

HEROES AND MARTYRS:

Joe Hill, Frank Little, and Wesley Everest

JUST AS ANY other human endeavor, the IWW had its strengths and its weaknesses. In its ranks were heroes and cowards, wise men and fools, selfless men and selfish ones. The IWW also had its martyrs; most of them bled and suffered anonymously. Thousands of Wobbly men and women were beaten, humiliated, degraded, tortured, jailed; some died for the cause and their beliefs.

No tally ever was made of the lives lost, the bodies broken, in that idealistic quest for a better world. Wobblies died courageously or cravenly, defiantly or suppliantly. They fell before gun, club, or the lyncher's rope. No record was made of their names; no one wept over their hidden graves; these were obscure fighters, scorned and mocked by the brutal men who struck them down in defilement of the flag the killers were claiming to protect.

Of all the Wobbly martyrs, only three found a place, however shadowy, in American folklore and legend. These were Frank Little, Wesley Everest, and Joe Hill. They were revered by the Wobblies as the tragic holy ones who had died that the IWW might live.

Joe Hill was the poet laureate of the IWW. The manner of his death had little to do with the Wobbly cause. He was tried, convicted, and sentenced to death for a sordid crime that had no connection with the movement.

Little and Everest died at the hands of lynch mobs, killed for their IWW activities. Yet, Little and Everest are almost forgotten today, while the name of Joe Hill lives on, celebrated in a famous folksong, "I Dreamed I Saw Joe Hill Last Night."

Frank Little, who once described himself as "half Indian, half white man, and all Wobbly," was a fiery, talented organizer, a member of the IWW General Executive Board (GEB), and one of the movement's outstanding leaders. While Wesley Everest, a lumberjack, was not so prominent in the IWW, his fellow workers respected him as a Wobbly. Although he hated war, Everest served with the U.S. Army in France and made a fine combat record.

Joe Hill's past is clouded. He claimed to have been born in Jevla, Sweden, in 1882. His real name was Joel Emmanuel Haaglung. Apparently, he came to the United States in 1901, Americanized his name to Joe Hillstrom, and then shortened it to Joe Hill. Almost nothing is known about Hill's early days in America. He seemed to have wandered about the country picking up odd jobs here and there. And everywhere he went, Joe Hill wrote songs and parodies that he put to popular melodies of the day or well-known hymns. Somehow, his songs caught on; passed from working stiff to bindle stiff, they soon were heard in every corner of the land.

The Wobblies adopted Hill's songs for their own. As they struggled to build the One Big Union and dreamed their "glorious dream," the Wobblies sang Joe Hill's songs. Somehow, these songs, "coarse as homespun and fine as silk," as the IWW poet and composer, Ralph Chaplin, described Hill's work, made the battle a little easier for the Wobbly warriors. Songs such as "Casey Jones," "The Union Scab," "The Rebel Girl," and "The Preacher and the Slave," were heard on picket lines, in demonstrations, in wheat fields and box cars, in lumber camps, mines, and mills.

There was irony in Joe Hill's death; it should have come in a fashion befitting a folk hero. Hill was arrested in January, 1914, for the murder of a grocer and his son. The prosecution claimed that he had committed the crime during an attempted holdup of the grocery store. The defense cried "Frame-up!" and argued that Hill was the victim of a plot by the businessmen of Salt Lake City because he had come there to organize for the IWW. Hill did nothing to help his own case. Recovering from a bullet wound at the time he was arrested, Hill alleged that he had been shot in a quarrel over a married woman. He revealed neither her name nor that of his assailant. The lady never came forward in his defense.

On Saturday night, January 10, 1914, John Morrison, the grocer, and his son, Alving, were murdered by one of two masked men who entered his store. Before dying, Morrison managed to fire one shot at the bandits as they fled. Some hours later, Hill turned up at a doctor's office seeking treatment of a bullet wound in his chest.

As he was obliged to do, the doctor, F. N. McHugh, reported Hill's visit to the police. He also informed them that his patient had been carrying an automatic pistol in a shoulder holster. The police connected Hill with the Morrison killings and arrested him. The gun Dr. McHugh had seen was never found. Kept in solitary confinement, charged with the murders of John and Alving Morrison, Hill waited five months for a trial.

Long before the court proceedings, local papers branded Hill guilty. One paper commented: "This man, Hill or Hillstrom, or whatever his true name, belongs to the IWW and freely admits it. . . . Everyone knows what crimes the IWW had committed in the past. If for no other reason than his membership in the IWW . . . Joe Hill must be guilty."

Hill's trial started on June 10, 1914, and concluded ten days later. The jury brought in the anticipated guilty verdict. The hearings had been marked by Hill's refusal to testify and an outburst during which he publicly fired the two volunteer lawyers who had accepted his case without fee. An IWW lawyer then took up his defense, but to no avail.

Amid mounting international protest, the verdict was appealed. Labor unions, churchmen, President Wilson, and even the king of Sweden called upon Utah's governor, William Spry, to show clemency, after Hill's appeals had been turned down by the U.S. Supreme Court. The best Spry would do was to grant a month's stay of execution until November 19, 1915.

At last the time ran out. Last-minute intervention by the White House brought from Spry a statement that "a further postponement at this time would be an unwarranted interference with the course of justice."

Hill received his death warrant calmly. On the last day, he sent a telegram to Big Bill Haywood: "Good-bye, Bill. I die like a true blue rebel. Don't waste time in mourning. Organize." Later that same day, a second telegram from Hill reached Haywood. It said in part: "Could you arrange to have my body hauled across the state line to be buried? I don't want to be found dead in Utah."

Big Bill replied: "Good-bye, Joe. You will live long in the hearts of the working class. Your songs will be sung wherever workers toil, urging them to organize."

At that time in Utah a condemned man had the choice between hanging or a firing squad—a hangover of the Old West. Hill picked the firing squad, which he faced without a blindfold. According to legend, he gave the command to fire. But this touch merely added to the Joe Hill myth. In dying, Hill gave the Wobblies a hero and a defiant slogan: "Don't mourn! Organize!"

A sense of uneasiness followed Hill's execution. Opinion questioned the wisdom of the act. On November 20, 1915, *The New York Times* asked editorially whether "Hill's death left an opening for people to make a hero of him . . . and might make him dead more dangerous to social stability than when he was alive."

The *Times* was wondering if Hill had become a martyr. The answer came a few days later when he was given a huge funeral in Chicago. More than 30,000 people wearing black armbands and marching to the beat of muffled drums paraded through the city to the cemetery where Hill was cremated. His ashes were placed in small envelopes and spread to the winds "in every state of the union and every country in the world," on May Day, 1916. Alive, Joe Hill merely had been a working-class poet and songsmith; dead, he became the symbol of revolution.

Although Joe Hill had died a "true-blue rebel," he was far less a real hero than Frank Little. Next to Big Bill Haywood, Frank Little was the most vital leader in the IWW.

No gifted orator, he matched Haywood in toughness, courage, and dedication. A Wobbly since 1906, Little had taken part in the free-speech fights at Missoula, Fresno, and Spokane. He organized lumberjacks, metal miners, and bindle stiffs all through the West and Southwest.

A member of the GEB by 1916, Little was a fierce advocate of direct action and opposed the First World War. When the conflict started in 1914, Wobbly leaders were not sure what course to follow, since most American workers favored the Allies. Although the IWW was against war in general, the GEB feared that open condemnation of both sides in the European hostilities would estrange the very workers the IWW was trying to organize.

If Haywood and other prominent Wobblies were unclear on their position, Frank Little knew precisely where he stood. Along with a few others on the GEB, Little issued a policy statement to the effect that the war was a capitalist plot that must be fought against even more vigorously than the economic, political, and social aspects of capitalism.

The divergent viewpoints within the IWW widened still further after the United States entered the war in April, 1917. The Wobblies hedged on their attitude to the draft, or whether members should refuse service in the armed forces and whether or not to strike in war industries.

For Frank Little there were no misgivings. "In principle . . . the IWW is opposed to war. . . . We therefore must do everything possible to end this one and to persuade workers not to join the army," he declared at a meeting of the GEB in June, 1917.

When Ralph Chaplin warned that such a stance might well "sound the death knell for the IWW," Little replied, "Better to go out in a blaze of glory than to knuckle down to the capitalists and their vile war."

Little's untimely death had nothing to do with his antiwar position. His murderers were not superpatriots, but hired agents of the Copper Trust paid to eliminate an effective IWW organizer. The fact that Little's antiwar statements had earned him many enemies enabled the killers to cloak themselves in an aura of patriotism. They had done the country a service by wiping out a foe of the United States, a traitor, a tool of the Kaiser.

Frank Little's life ended in Butte, Montana, where he was leading a strike of copper miners against the Anaconda Copper Company. Little, who recently had broken a leg, addressed a Butte strike rally on the night of July 31, 1917. With his leg in a cast, he delivered a fighting talk to the miners and shouted defiance at company guards threatening him with rifles and pistols.

At midnight, he returned to his room at the Finn Hotel in Butte. About a half-hour later, six masked, armed men broke into Little's room, slugged him, and dragged the stunned Wobbly behind their car along a rutted dirt road to the Milwaukee Railroad trestle a few miles from town.

There they hanged Frank Little from the railroad bridge and pinned a crudely lettered placard to his body: "First and Last Warning!" The barbarity of the lynching shocked the people of Butte, the labor movement, and the American public. Telegrams of protest poured in to the city officials; the local police put on a big show of searching for the killers, but failed to arrest anyone.

Thus, Frank Little died for the cause he loved, only to be forgotten through the years.

The third Wobbly martyr was not a leader, not even well known, but a simple red-card bearer named Wesley Everest, a lumberjack. Although a Wobbly to the core, Everest enlisted in the army, went to France with the American Expeditionary Force (AEF) as a doughboy, fought in the trenches, and returned to the States in the fall of 1919.

That November, Everest was in Centralia, Washington, during a protracted lumber strike. The lumber bosses issued a statement from their association headquarters in Centralia warning the IWW to "clear out of town or be carried out in a hearse." On November 11, 1919, the first anniversary of the Armistice, the Centralia post of the American Legion mobilized its members and marched upon the IWW meeting hall. Some of the Legionnaires carried rifles and shotguns; others were armed with pistols, clubs, and lengths of lead pipe. As the head of the parade approached the hall, shots rang out. The Legionnaires, outnumbering the Wobblies, rushed the building. In the ensuing battle three of the ex-soldiers were killed.

Among the few defending the hall was Wesley Everest wearing his doughboy uniform. "I fought for democracy in

France, and I'm going to fight for it here," he said, taking up a rifle and .45-caliber pistol.

When the Legion men broke into the building, Everest cried, "Stand where you are! I'll kill the first one who moves." Instead of obeying him, the infuriated Legionnaires charged. Everest calmly emptied the rifle into the onsurging crowd, dropped it, drew the pistol, and fled through the back door into the woods, the mob at his heels.

He ran for the Skookumchuck River, tried to wade it, but found the current too strong. Waist deep in water, he turned on his pursuers and shouted, "Get the cops! I'll surrender to the cops, but not to any of you!"

A man named Dale Hubbard, the nephew of the lumber association head in Centralia, yelled, "Don't listen to that damned red! Get him! Come on! Follow me!"

As the mob closed in on him, Everest snapped off four shots. The first bullet killed Hubbard. The Wobbly fought with his fists until he was overpowered and dragged to shore. "We're going to string you up!" a Legionnaire shouted.

"You haven't the guts to hang a man in daylight!" Everest sneered.

He was right.

That mob did not finish him off then. Instead, he was hauled to jail; but after dark, the electricity in Centralia suddenly failed. A band of hooded men smashed in the jailhouse door, wrested the keys from the deputy on duty, and opened Everest's cell.

"Tell the boys I died for my class!" the lumberjack cried as the lynchers carried him off.

They carted him to the Chehalis River Bridge, mutilated him, then hanged him and riddled his body with bullets. His corpse was cut down and buried in an unmarked grave.

The Everest lynching was followed by unbridled terror against the Wobblies in Washington State. Hundreds of them were arrested and eleven held for shooting the three Legionnaires at the Centralia IWW hall. Six Wobblies were sentenced to terms of twenty-five to forty years in the state penitentiary.

In 1923, nine of the jurors swore under oath that they had reached their verdict under pressure from the lumber bosses and that no one on the jury actually believed the convicted Wobblies had been guilty.

The Centralia trial broke the back of the IWW in Washington, but it left a trail of guilty consciences behind. Not until the 1930's did the imprisoned men finally obtain justice. An impartial investigation concluded that the "six IWW men in Walla Walla Penitentiary . . . were unfairly tried and convicted." By 1934, the men were pardoned. The price they paid was steep—fifteen years in prison, but their sacrifice did not match Wesley Everest's; they still were alive.

The fate of the Centralia Six and Wesley Everest epitomized the persecutions borne by the entire IWW after America's entry into the Great War.

THE WAR, PERSECUTION A LINGERING END AND HOPE

THE APRIL 14, 1917, issue of *The Industrial Worker,* the IWW's newspaper, contained a poem by an anonymous contributor. Entitled "I Love My Flag," it began:

> I love my flag, I do, I do,
> Which floats upon the breeze.
> I also love my arms and legs,
> And neck and nose and knees.
> One little shell might spoil them all
> Or give them such a twist
> They would be of no use to me
> I guess I won't enlist.

It was this sort of antiwar sentiment that the IWW had stressed in the past. Yet when America went to war, that attitude isolated the Wobblies from the American working class.

The country was swept by a wave of patriotism in April, 1917. But the Wobblies refused to give up their efforts on behalf of the workers, even if this meant advocating strikes in industries vital to the war effort.

"We are unalterably opposed to war and conscription," a Wobbly leader wrote. "Had we the power, we would stop every ship, train, mine and mill, every food and supply plant, every wheel of industry."

However, the IWW lacked the power for this ambitious antiwar, antidraft policy. The war violated every Wobbly principle, but even Big Bill Haywood admitted, "I am at a loss as to definite steps to be taken against the war." He also said, "I believe . . . that the world war is of small importance compared to the great class war. . . . We shall continue to fight for the emancipation of the working class, despite all other circumstances."

War or no war, the IWW's GEB decided to continue its activities in certain key industries and in the agricultural field. The Wobblies led strikes in copper mines and timber lands, concentrating in Arizona, Montana, and on the West Coast. Although there was no evidence that the IWW strikes were for any reason other than better pay and working conditions, a cry of "Treason!" went up from politicians, businessmen, and the newspapers. The Wobblies were smeared as pro-German and one Arizona senator announced that the letters IWW stood for "Imperial Wilhelm's Warriors." (Wilhelm I was the German Kaiser.)

Included in the pro-German actions that the IWW purportedly carried out was a mass demonstration against the draft in Oklahoma. During August, 1917, two hundred farmers from a 35,000-member group called the Workingman's Union, marched on Sasakwa, Oklahoma, armed with rifles, to destroy the induction center there.

The incident, known as the Green Corn Rebellion, ended without a shot fired. Faced by state police, the marchers, led by an ex-Wobbly, quietly surrendered. The leader, Rube

Munson, was jailed for ten years. Lesser offenders received five-year sentences and the rank-and-file Green Corn Rebels served a year and a day in a federal penitentiary.

The Green Corn Rebellion, the timber and copper strikes, and several other instances of civil disorder fanned the belief that the IWW was a "hotbed of German agents" and that "Berlin gold" was financing the Wobbly attempts to hamstring America's war efforts.

In a calmer period, cooler heads would possibly have prevailed, but the nation was at war, the public aroused to patriotic fervor. Daily the newspapers drummed the idea that the IWW was subversive and treasonable. The Cleveland *News* insisted: "While we are at war, the only room we can afford the IWW is behind prison walls."

Reckless news stories spread hysterical lies about the Wobblies. The papers accused them of poisoning reservoirs, plotting to burn cities and farms, sabotaging railroads, and contaminating the national meat supply. A North Dakota paper stated: "This foul breed of subhuman criminal . . . the so-called Wobbly . . . lives by knife, bomb and torch. . . . He knows only how to kill, burn and destroy."

An editorial in the Tulsa, Oklahoma, *Daily World,* went beyond all limits of reason. It stated in part:

> The first step in whipping the Germans is to strangle the IWWs. Kill them just as you would kill any other kind of snake. . . . It is no time to waste money on trials and things like that. All that is necessary is the evidence and a firing squad!

With such talk whipping up public unrest, Washington was besieged to "do something about the IWW." President Woodrow Wilson acted in September, 1917, appointing Judge Harry J. Covington as head of a special committee to investigate the IWW.

Although Big Bill Haywood, as secretary-treasurer of the IWW, notified Covington that he would supply all requested files, Department of Justice agents launched nationwide raids against the Wobblies on September 5, 1917. The raiders smashed into IWW headquarters, kicked down doors, forced open file cabinets, rifled desks and safes, and caused considerable physical damage to the premises. On this day of the "Big Pinch," the federals seized five tons of letters, newspapers, propaganda pamphlets, minutes of meetings, badges, buttons, stickers, dues books, and membership cards.

After sifting through this mountain of material, the Department of Justice announced that it had sufficient evidence to indict the IWW as a "treasonable and criminal conspiracy which opposed by force the execution of the laws of the United States and obstructed the prosecution of the war."

On September 28, 1917, 184 IWW leaders were arrested at various points in the country and hit with charges ranging from hampering the war effort to spreading sedition in the armed forces. The prisoners were tried in three separate groups at Chicago, Sacramento, and Wichita, Kansas.

The first of the cases was heard in Chicago Federal Court before Judge Kenesaw Mountain Landis on April 1, 1918. One hundred and one Wobblies, charged with conspiracy, sabotage, and obstruction of the war effort, were the defendants. Much interest centered on this trial, for Big Bill Haywood was one of the accused.

Jack Reed, of the Paterson Pageant fame, covered the proceedings for *The Masses*, a leftist magazine. Reed had come a long way since 1913; he now was a world-famous journalist, war correspondent, and author. He had been in Russia during the 1917 November Revolution and would soon publish his best-known book, *Ten Days That Shook the*

World, a firsthand account of the Bolshevik revolt in Petrograd.

Reed wrote of Judge Landis: "Small on the huge bench sits a wasted man with untidy white hair, an emaciated face in which two burning eyes are set like jewels, parchment skin split by a crack of a mouth; the face of Andrew Jackson three years dead. . . ."

The Wobbly trial lasted nearly five months until the end of August, 1918. Defense Attorney George Vanderveer called 61 witnesses to the stand, including Haywood, who made a good impression on almost everyone with his testimony. One Wobbly witness, Red Doran, finished a long stint on the stand by turning to the jury and saying, "It is customary for IWW speakers to take up a collection, but under the circumstances, I think we will dispense with it." Defendants, prosecution, judge, jury, and spectators roared with laughter at Doran's sally.

After Doran was through, there remained very little to laugh about. In vain, Vanderveer tried to disprove government charges that the IWW was hampering the war effort. He pointed to the number of Wobblies in the army and to the fact that there had been no strikes or work stoppages among IWW longshoremen who loaded ships bound for the war zone.

After weeks of testimony from both sides, the case went to the jury on August 30, 1918. Within an hour the jurors returned with a verdict of "Guilty" on all counts. A large crowd waiting outside the courtroom cheered the findings. In the street, a throng applauded the verdict and a band played patriotic airs.

It had not mattered to the jury that Haywood, Doran, and the rest had spoken feelingly of the better world the IWW sought—a world without poverty, ignorance, exploitation, and misery; a world in which all men would be treated as brothers and equals. The jurors had chosen to believe that the defendants were raging revolutionaries, firebrands, foresworn to overturn established society and replace it with anarchy.

That same day, Judge Landis passed sentence on the defendants. Fifteen of them received twenty-year terms; thirty-five were given ten years, thirty-three got five years, and thirteen a year and a day. On top of this, the prisoners were fined a total of $2,300,000.

In the street, a cordon of police struggled with jeering crowds as the manacled Wobblies were led from the courthouse. Surrounded by armed guards and mounted police, they were marched to the La Salle Street Railroad Station, where a special train was getting up steam to carry them to Leavenworth Prison. Although shaken by the stiff sentences imposed on them, the Wobblies were not crushed; they marched with heads high singing "Solidarity Forever!"

The men being tried in Sacramento and Wichita fared no better than did the Chicago group. After a period in prison before trial, they all were found guilty and sentenced to long terms.

The Sacramento Wobblies stood mute, offering no defense, and saying nothing, during their six-week-long trial. Only after sentence had been passed did one of their number, Fred Esmond, speak out. He said, in part:

> I am not asking for mercy. I'll take neither mercy nor pity from you or any representative of this government. . . . I want to go on record . . . as saying that we, the outcasts, have been framed, clubbed, beaten, slugged, martyred and murdered. . . . Is it any wonder that I do not consider myself bound by your procedure, when this court and its proceedings are a disgrace to the United States? You have done more than any IWW could possibly do to drag your Stars and Stripes through the mire.

The worst ordeal was experienced by the thirty-four Wobblies being held in Wichita, Kansas. Arrested in November, 1917, they were not tried until December, 1919. For two years and one month they suffered intolerable jail conditions. Guards beat them at the slightest provocation; even a minor infraction of regulations by a Wobbly brought him seven days on bread and water in solitary. A jailer boasted to a newsman, "We know how to keep those troublemakers in line. When one of them squawks we go in and kick his guts out. . . ."

Each of the Wichita Wobblies fell sick in prison. Several died of tuberculosis. Two went mad. The trial was a travesty. After staying out only a few minutes, the jury came in with a guilty verdict. Terms ranging from one to nine years at Leavenworth were meted out to the men. (The Sacramento group received similar harsh treatment and joined the rest at Leavenworth.)

Just before the Wichita Wobblies went on trial, the United States was caught up in a full-scale, country-wide Red Scare, initiated by Attorney General Mitchell Palmer, in November, 1919. An ambitious man, Palmer had his eye on the White House. He took advantage of an unseemly incident to boost himself into public notice. Early in November, someone planted a bomb under the porch of Palmer's residence. It exploded without causing casualties or damage, but the attorney general exploited the occurrence to the fullest. Claiming that the bomb had been the signal for a red uprising, Palmer announced that he was going to wipe out that menace forever. Armed with special antisedition powers given the attorney general in 1918 by Congress, Palmer unleashed an unprecedented wave of antiradical attacks.

In what were to become infamous as the "Palmer Raids," federal agents broke into headquarters of radical groups in eighteen cities. They had no warrants to search the premises or to arrest individuals but did both. This offensive, launched on November 7, 1919, coincided with the second anniversary of the Communist revolution in Russia. It was the first in a series of similar invasions that lasted well into 1920 and did not end until 10,000 radicals of all shadings had been arrested. Foreign-born socialists, Wobblies, and other dissenters were deported. One ship, loaded with 250 deportees, was dubbed "The Red Ark" by newsmen.

Palmer's crusade petered out after several months. Americans were growing weary of headlines about the "Red Menace." Some newspapers lambasted Palmer as a demagogue. The attorney general, a Quaker, had labeled himself the "Fighting Quaker"; his newspaper critics changed that to the "Quaker Faker."

Despite all Palmer's efforts to keep it alive, the Red Scare abated, but the damage had been done. Although the American people finally had rejected political repression, their change of attitude did not save many thousands from needless persecution and did not help those whose lives and careers had been wrecked by Palmer.

The IWW was the greatest casualty of the attorney general's campaign. It not only was depleted numerically, but also ruined financially by the Palmer Raids and the "Wobbly Trials." Fearful of consequences, thousands of members tore up their red cards; only the most courageous and most dedicated were prepared to "face the music" for belonging to the IWW. Apparently, the fortunes of the Wobblies could sink no lower; yet even worse befell them.

IWW attorneys appealed the verdict of the Chicago case, and while the U.S. Court of Appeals was biding its decision, Big Bill Haywood and eight other top leaders were let out of prison on bail that totaled more than $100,000. In October, 1920, the Court of Appeals upheld the verdict. Haywood and the rest were ordered to surrender and return to Leavenworth.

Instead, Haywood and his eight companions, using falsified passports, fled to Russia. Debilitated by diabetes, his eyesight failing, Haywood had succumbed to the blandishments of the newly formed American Communist Party, whose leaders had persuaded him that his place was in Russia to help Lenin overthrow world capitalism.

Big Bill was warmly greeted in Moscow. He was put in charge of a workers' colony in the Kuznetsk Basin region of the Soviet Union. His flight was a crushing blow to the IWW rank and filers. The ordinary Wobbly never forgave Big Bill for this desertion. Otto Christensen, the attorney who had taken the IWW case to the Court of Appeals, denounced Haywood as a "despicable coward and . . . traitor. . . . His craven act will harm the cause of amnesty for political prisoners. Certainly, he will be disowned by the IWW and its sympathizers."

The nine bail-jumpers cost the IWW a great deal of money. The $100,000 needed to repay the bondsmen was raised by individual contributions. "We're handing over this money, not for Haywood, but to save the honor of the IWW," a group of Colorado miners wrote.

Haywood's life in Russia was neither fruitful nor happy. The Kuznetsk Basin project fizzled out. He returned to Moscow in 1928, a desolate, lonely old man. In May of that year he died. His ashes were divided for burial between the Kremlin wall and the Waldheim Cemetery in Chicago, next to the graves of the Haymarket martyrs.

The IWW never recovered from the post-World War I persecutions, although by 1924 most of the Wobblies in federal prisons had been granted amnesty.

Some condemned the Wobblies as rebels; some scorned them for being "shiftless" and "rootless"; but nobody could deny their courage—even the worst enemies of the IWW admitted that the Wobblies had "guts."

In a day when social justice and industrial democracy were throttled by greedy men, the Wobblies fought for liberty and decency. They marched to a different drummer, working class zealots who never doubted that right was on their side. Ralph Chaplin summed up the Wobbly creed in the closing verse of his song, "Solidarity Forever!":

> In our hands is placed a power greater than their hoarded gold;
> Greater than the might of armies, magnified a thousand fold.
> We can bring to birth the new world from the ashes of the old,
> For the Union makes us strong.

The Wobblies did not succeed in bringing to "birth the new world from the ashes of the old," but they did sire a new era of industrial unionism during the 1930's, when the CIO rose to challenge the AFL.

In the mid-30's, while the Depression still throttled the United States, advocates of industrial unionism within the AFL broke away under the leadership of John L. Lewis and others to "organize the unorganized." They built unions along industrial—not craft—lines. Although the men who originally formed the CIO rarely gave credit to the IWW, the CIO owes its existence to the legacy left by the Wobblies.

Even in its direct action tactics, the CIO stole a page from the IWW, by resorting to the sitdown strike as the Wobblies first had done in 1905. That action so disturbed the balance between labor and management that it was subsequently outlawed by Congress.

Today, the IWW exists mainly in memory; even the songs of the Wobblies are seldom heard, but because they long ago fought for what were then considered "radical" ideas, American labor has reaped the benefits won in the pioneer struggles led by the IWW.

Big Bill and the rest are gone; time has obscured their names, but every gain made by labor belongs to those forgotten men who stood for the freedom and dignity of the American worker.

A BRIEF GLOSSARY OF IWW SLANG

Anchor A pick
Banjo A short-handled shovel
Benny An overcoat
Bindle A bed roll in which a bindle stiff carries his belongings
Bindle stiff A worker who carries a bindle
Boiler A cook who never bakes or fries but boils food
Bull A police officer
Buy a master To pay a fee to an employment shark for a job
California blankets Newspapers used for a blanket
Can Police station
Carrying the banner Staying awake all night to avoid paying for lodging: walking the streets, dozing in a subway, going to an all-night movie, sitting up in a bus or railroad station
Cat A worker who does his job well. A "hep cat." "Cat" also applies to certain types of work: a "straw" cat, for example, works in hay fields. "Cat" is another term for sabotage. "Turn the cat loose" means to commit an act of sabotage
Chow Food
Chuck Cooked food; as a verb, "chuck" means to throw
Clam-gun Shovel for digging clams

Coin Money
Crummy Lousy
Deck Roof or floor of a passenger train
Dick Detective
Dingbat A homeless, harmless, helpless tramp
Drag Street
Dump A hangout
Enlightened Informed, educated, intelligent, class-conscious
Fallers Loggers who fell trees
Fanned Hit on the soles by a police nightstick
Fellow Worker Term by which Wobblies addressed one another
Fink Strikebreaker, informer
Fish Jail term for new prisoner
Flip To board a train in motion
Fritz, on the In bad shape
Gandy dancer Worker on railroad gang, a track walker
Gay cat A hobo
Glim Match, a light, or eyes
Gut robber Stingy cook
Handout A lunch in a brown paper bag
Harness bull Uniformed policeman
Harp An Irishman
Harvest stiff Migratory agricultural worker
Highball Fast
Hijack Hold up
Hit the ball Work at faster than normal pace
Hobo Migratory worker
Hoosier An incompetent
Hoosier up To act incompetently on purpose
Hurry buggy A patrol wagon
Idiot Stick A shovel
Jake Satisfactory
Java Coffee
John Farmer
Jungle Meeting place of hoboes
Kicks Shoes
Knowledge box Schoolhouse
Live One A worker with money

Lump Food acquired by begging
Lush A drunkard
Make a riffle Get money for a meal or lodging by begging
Mancatcher Employment agent
Mark A person from whom it is easy to get money
Moniker Name or nickname
Moocher A beggar
Muck Any material to be shoveled
Muck stick Long-handled shovel
Mulligan Stew
Mulligan mixer A cook
Nose bag Lunch pail
OBU Initials of One Big Union
On the hog Broke
Packing the rigging Carrying Wobbly literature
Panhandling Begging on streets
Parasite Labor's class enemy
Pearl diver Dishwasher
Peddler Slow freight
Plute Short for plutocrat
Pot latch A party, a social affair
Pulled out Left town
Pusher A boss
Rattler A fast freight train
Rebel A class-conscious worker opposing capitalism
Rods Drawrods beneath a freight train. Hence: "ride the rods"
Rummy A drunk
Rustling Getting busy to find food or lodgings
Sap A police nightstick
Scab A strikebreaker
Scissorbill A worker who is not class-conscious
Sewer hog A ditch digger
Shark An employment agent
Sheets Newspapers
Shorthorn Young man
Slave A wage earner
Sloughed Arrested
Smilo joint A speakeasy or tavern selling bootleg liquor

Snipe A cigarette butt
Stiff Any kind of migrant worker; a corpse
Straw boss Foreman
Taking five Knocking off work for five minutes
Throw the guts Talk freely
Timber beasts Lumberjacks
Timber wolves Lumberjacks
Tin horn A petty gambler or person
Town clown A village constable
Traipse To travel around
Trap A mouth
Ukulele A short-handled shovel
Vag A vagrant
Wobbly A member of the IWW
Yegg A safecracker
Yellow legs Mounted police or United States Cavalry

BIBLIOGRAPHY

ALTHOUGH MUCH of the research for *Pie in the Sky* was gleaned from newspapers, magazines, personal reminiscences, and pamphlets, a number of books, available to the general reader, were helpful. For a general history of the IWW, I found Patrick Henshaw's *The Wobblies* an excellent work. *Rebel Voices*, edited by Joyce L. Kornbluh, contains a solid history of the IWW, pictures, songs, biographies, and writings of Wobbly leaders as well as rank and filers. It probably is the best all-around reference on the subject.

A brief paperback, *The IWW. Its First Fifty Years* (1905–1955), compiled by Fred Thompson, is a splendid capsule of the Wobbly story.

Good background is provided in *The Autobiography of Big Bill Haywood,* which delves into the IWW as seen by its Founding Father. Elizabeth Gurley Flynn's memoir, *I Speak My Own Piece* deals compellingly not only with the IWW but also with the radical movement as a whole. *The Life of Mother Jones,* written in 1925, when that grand old lady of labor was ninety-five years old, tells of her role in the building of One Big Union. John Reed's role in the Paterson Strike is told in *The Lost*

Revolutionary, by Richard O'Connor and Dale L. Walker. This is a well-done biography of John Reed.

For a background on the American labor movement, I immodestly refer my young readers to my own book, *The Great Struggle: Labor In America. Nineteen Nineteen*, a novel by John Dos Passos, gives a stirring picture of the life and times of the Wobblies.

INDEX

Werstein

Pie in the sky, an American struggle, the Wobblies and their times

DATE DUE

MAR 16			
APR 11 '72			
APR 28 '72			
MAY 12 '72			
MAY 23 1973			
NOV 8 1973			
MAY 3 '76			
MAY 5 1976			
APR 21 1977			
MAY 1 1978			
MAY 8 1979			
MAY 17 1979			
MAY 25 1979			
MAR 3 '80			
MAY 7 1981			
APR 22 '85			